To Margarete, my mother,
and Alex and Jaclyn, my granddaughters,
who embody the boundaries of my present family system

Contents

YOUR FAMILY YOUR SELF

How to Analyze Your Family System
to Understand Yourself, & Achieve More
Satisfying Relationships with Your Loved Ones

WILLIAM BLEVINS

NEW HARBINGER PUBLICATIONS, INC.

Publisher's Note

This publication is designed to provide accurate and authoritative information in regard to the subject matter covered. It is sold with the understanding that the publisher is not engaged in rendering psychological, financial, legal, or other professional services. If expert assistance or counseling is needed, the services of a competent professional should be sought.

Library of Congress Catalog Number: 93-084714
ISBN 1-879237-53-9 Paperback
ISBN 1-879237-54-7 Hardcover

Copyright © by William L. Blevins
                    New Harbinger Publications, Inc.
                    5674 Shattuck Avenue
                    Oakland, CA 94609

Printed in the United States of America on recycled paper.

Cover design by SHELBY DESIGNS & ILLUSTRATES, cover art by Phil Cheung

First printing 1993, 5,000 copies

Acknowledgments

I have been a Marriage and Family Therapist for over 15 years and a family member all my life. Both the profession and the clan kindle my profound interest in the impact that family dynamics has upon the development of personality. At this point in my own personal and professional journey, I no longer believe that people enter this world with a fully intact, but undeveloped, personality. People do begin life with a genetic package and a set of emotional predispositions, or computer hardware, as Sam Keen once called it; yet the biological and emotional packages do not include all of the personality idiosyncrasies that evolve over the years. I believe that many of these idiosyncrasies are contextual. They emerge from the constant interaction with, and dependence upon, significant others in our lives. This book issues in part from a personal quest to discover my identity within the context of my own ancestry, and in part from a course I teach called "Search For Yourself," designed to teach people how to discover themselves by exploring their original family.

Although my name appears on the cover, this book is not the product of my labor alone. I am indebted to my students, clients, and colleagues. They continually expand my understanding of what being human means by sharing their own lives with me. I am grateful for every member of my nuclear and extended family. Each member in his or her own way has helped to "call me into being," especially my children, Suzanne and Chuck, Art and Mary Lisa, Alan, and Kym. My wife Carolyn has quietly endured my long hours with the computer in churning out this text. She facilitated the whole process with her patience, encouragement, and candid suggestions.

Edra Garrett Cureton enabled me to remain focused on this project by her tireless efforts in handling many of the essentials that nurture writing. She kept watch over my schedule, helped in doing research, performed corollary writing tasks without a whimper, and assisted in preparing the final manuscript.

I am especially appreciative of everyone at New Harbinger who had a hand in this publication. Patrick Fanning's favorable comments and interest in publishing the book were most encouraging. Barbara Quick, my editor, has been insightful, skillful, and right. Her suggestions about this or that in the text were right more often than mine. I appreciate her work throughout the whole process, especially since she balanced her professional assignments with the new demands of motherhood. And I thank Gayle Zanca and Mary Lee Cole for their expertise in the production and marketing strategies of the finished product.

Most of the case illustrations used in this book are based upon real persons and experiences, although I have carefully concealed all identifying factors to ensure anonymity. Some of the illustrations are composites of situations which commonly occur in family experiences. I am exceedingly grateful to the clients who permitted me to use portions of their story, as well as to all the people who allowed me the privilege of sharing their lives and struggles.

Prologue

In ancient Greece, few mythical heroes were more admired than Theseus. According to the story, Aegeus, king of Athens, had no son to inherit his throne. He had 50 nephews who aspired to the position, but Aegeus wanted a son of his own. He traveled a great distance to consult an oracle about this matter. On his way home, Aegeus interrupted his journey to accept the hospitality of Pittheus, king of Troezen. While there, Aegeus fell in love with Aethra, Pittheus's daughter. They were married and soon after Aethra conceived a child. Although there was a rumor that the child belonged to Poseidon, Aegeus believed himself to be the father. He did not, however, want to bring his wife and unborn child to Athens. He feared that his nephews might kill the child if it were a male.

Before his return to Athens, Aegeus placed his sword and a pair of sandals under a large rock. He instructed Aethra, in the event she gave birth to a son, to raise the boy in Troezen until he was old enough to remove the rock and retrieve the sword and sandals. At that time, she was to disclose the secret of his family heritage and send him to Athens.

In time, Aethra did give birth to a son, Theseus, and raised him in her father's house. Theseus distinguished himself with feats of strength even as a child. When he was 16, Aethra considered him mature enough to join his father. She took him to the rock, which he moved with very little effort, and he reclaimed the sword and the sandals. Aethra then revealed the secret of his identity and sent him to his father.

Although his mother urged him to travel by sea to Athens, which was the safer route, Theseus chose to go by land, a way that was infested with robbers and vicious animals. These dangers did indeed threaten Theseus's life, but he overcame all of them.

When Theseus arrived in Athens he was preceded by his reputation as a destroyer of monsters. Aegeus, his father, was now married to a sorceress, Medea, who intuited Theseus's true identity without disclosing it to the king. She convinced him that the young man was a potential menace. Medea persuaded the king to invite Theseus to a banquet on the pretext of honoring him, but in reality to poison him. Even though this plot violated the Greek custom of hospitality, the king consented to her plan. During the banquet, Aegeus noticed Theseus's sword and recognized it as his own. Realizing that this was his son, Aegeus knocked over the cup of poison just before it was offered to Theseus and joyfully proclaimed his identity to all the assembled company. Medea was sent into exile.

Theseus is a model for people who want to claim their own identity and personal destiny. These are everyone's birthrights. Theseus uncovered the secret of his identity and destiny in two ways: by recovering the artifacts hidden under the rock and by his deeds of courage. Reclaiming the sword and sandals of his father signified the disclosure of who Theseus really was. His identity was inseparably connected to his family heritage. His exploits of heroism in slaying monsters that threatened human life—especially the Minotaur in Crete and the bull at Marathon—symbolized Theseus's mastery over the animal passions that lurked deep inside his own being. Only as people conquer these destructive inner forces can they achieve their potential destiny.

The story of Theseus wielding the sword and wearing his father's sandals teaches that individuals claim their real identity and grasp their destiny when they reconnect with their ancestral heritage, a heritage that meanders through the labyrinth of their family origins. This fact is as old as humanity itself. It is as true today as it was in ancient times. You discover who you are when you know your own people. You understand your destiny—the script you are living—when you identify the themes and issues ingrained in your original family system. This is so because you were not spawned in a vacuum. You are a unique expression of a family system that extends backwards across numerous generations. The sword and the sandals represent the personal generational legacy that connects you to the past. Only when you reclaim your past are you able to solve the mystery of your own being. This is because the quality of your present life is fashioned by the interplay of conscious and unconscious forces generated in your family of origin.

Introduction

Chameleons are charming diminutive lizards that fascinate people by their ability to change colors. They assume the color of whatever they happen to be resting on. Have you ever wondered what the world would be like if humans could do the same thing? To make this possibility even more intriguing, what if humans took the physical appearance of whomever their thoughts and feelings belonged to? If you happened to believe something your father believes, you'd look like your father whenever you thought of that belief. If you felt the way your mother wanted you to feel about something, you'd look like your mother whenever you felt that particular emotion. If you adopted an opinion of one of your peers, you'd look like that person whenever you affirmed that opinion. According to this fantasy, you would look like yourself only when you were thinking your own thoughts, believing your own beliefs, affirming your own opinions, and living your own life. If this fantasy were real, how often would you look like yourself? How frequently would you appear as someone else?

To some degree, human beings do have a chameleonlike ability. There are numerous occasions when people feel one way inside, but act another way outside (Jourard, 1964). Fritz Perls, the father of Gestalt therapy, defines this as living on an "as if" level of existence (Fagan and Shepherd, 1970). You function on this level when you are scared on the inside, but behave as if you were feeling brave. The same is true on those occasions when you are really angry, but act as if you weren't. There are other times when you are bored by something, but act as if you were genuinely interested. Or I may dislike you, but behave as if I love you. When people function on the *as if* level, they can never truly be who they are.

Human beings have an uncommon ability to mask their inner reality. You may be skillful at masquerading your real self so that others do not know who you really are. Some people are so adept at this practice that they thoroughly bewilder themselves. These people have difficulty distinguishing who they are from how they appear. At any given moment, they have trouble knowing exactly what they themselves think, feel, or desire. Not only are these people misunderstood by others—they don't even know themselves.

I have a poster hanging on my office door with the message: *He who trims himself to suit everybody will soon whittle himself away.*

This message is compelling for me, because I have spent much of my life being who others wanted me to be. I have spoken what others wanted to hear. I have believed what others have professed. I have disguised my emotions to protect the feelings of others. And I have sculpted my behavior to conform to others' expectations. Now, after years of fabricating this public image, I have some nagging questions about myself. Am I really the person I've fashioned for others? Or am I someone else merely playing that role? Maybe I'm a composite of the public image and a private self that lurks in the shadows. But then again, is my supposed private self any more real than the public image? Who am I really? How much of me is the *me* I perform for others? How much of me is the *me* I have borrowed from others? And how much of me is the real *me*, if any? When I think about it, the questions concerning my identity are as complicated and puzzling as they are intriguing. Yet I continue to ask them of myself because I truly want to discover who lives on the inside of me.

Identifying the real me is a difficult task. Like firmly grasping a wet bar of soap, it's a slippery business. Often, when I think I've got a secure grip on some genuine part of me, the part slips through my fingers, and I realize that it's only another feature that I've taken from someone else. Is there a real me? And if there is, how do I find myself? I've been told that, like everyone else in the world, I am unique. If this is true, why is so much of me merely absorbed from what others believe, expect, and desire? Where does the *me* defined by others end and my own uniqueness begin?

The message I hear is that there's never been anyone exactly like me in the history of mankind, nor will there ever be. I am created to be unlike everyone else. I have my own fingerprints, voiceprint, and blend of DNA. Yet, if it is true that I am unique, why are others so uncomfortable when I'm different? Why are others uneasy when I'm just being myself? Why do others need to define me the way they want? If I was created to be a distinctive self, why am I pressured to trim myself to suit everybody else? Discovering who I really am is not only slippery, it's risky. Others challenge my efforts to be myself. That's why I'm mostly acceptable only when I am the person they want me to be.

For years, being who others wanted brought a desirable tranquility. Pleasing others produced acceptance and approval. I received plaudits by tailoring my ideas to others' beliefs. This was easier than thinking for myself, and it was safer than defending my own positions. I achieved professionally by following road maps drawn by other travelers. I found pleasure in dancing to the tunes piped by whomever my audience happened to be. But now, all of that has changed. Being who others want me to be doesn't make me feel tranquil, nor does it seem desirable. For myself, others' maps are only a maze and their tunes no longer inspire me to dance. After years of fabricating a self for others, I have a passion to chart my own map and write my own music. I want to peel away the cultural layers that obscure my unique self and be my own person. And deep inside, I know that I'm the only one who can make this search. I am the only person who can discover me.

The desire to find myself is shrouded in mystery. Why, at this stage of life, do I pursue this quest? Maybe it is motivated by middle age. Being for others is fine when there are many years ahead. Yet it is not so pleasant when there are fewer years left. Or maybe the quest was generated by my father's death. Accepting my own mortality involves identifying who I really am. Or maybe the wish to uncover my real self is merely the natural outcome of developing as an authentic human being. If there is an inner force that drives an acorn to become an oak tree or a seed to become a plant, is there a natural lifeforce that nudges people to actualize their potential selves? Or maybe my quest results from the last child leaving home. For 32 years, I have played various family roles—provider, father, disciplinarian, teacher, and the like. With no more kids in the nest, I must now redefine myself. The old roles are archaic and no longer have any meaning.

Whatever motivates my search, I can ignore the quest for selfhood only at my own peril. If I am ever to live before I die, I must discover who I really am. How do I do that? Where does the journey begin, and what direction does it take? There are many leads to follow. I can take psychological inventories that measure intelligence, personality traits, natural abilities, talents, and so forth, but paper and pencil tests only trace the fringes of myself. They tend to measure as much of my fabricated image as they do my real self, and they don't penetrate to the core of my being. I can process feedback from friends and acquaintances about myself, yet their data mostly describe the roles I've played. I can twist into a lotus position and contemplate my own navel, searching for my elusive identity in the recesses of my own unconsciousness. Yet how can I be sure that I will not simply rethink what I already know? Where do I look to discover *me*? It's a knotty question.

How much of *you* is you, and how much of *you* is someone else? How much of *me* is really me and not someone else? From experience as a marriage and family therapist, college professor, minister, and human being, I believe that people can discover themselves by exploring their own families. The embryo of your real self is enveloped in the womb of your original family. Your family of origin gave you birth and cradled your development as a person. Your family system governed your behavior and provided a script for you to follow. Your family system also joined you to previous generations, both biologically and emotionally. Whatever else may be true about your identity, you were not born in a vacuum. You are part of a larger family that has shaped your life from the moment of conception. Although people normally define themselves as a singular individual, each one of us is a plural. You are inseparably connected to a family unit. For this reason, if you are ever to discover your self, you will do so by probing the secret passages and hidden tunnels that meander back and forth through the recesses of your generational heritage. Exploring your family is an expedition that inevitably leads to the discovery of your self.

In his book, *Your Mythic Journey*, Sam Keen suggests that you often live out the unconscious fears of your parents. I agree with him, but, as he suggests, that is not the whole story. Your life script is shaped by numerous other elements embedded in your own family. Portions of your script originate from unconscious issues that are passed from one generation to another. Other parts of that script derive from assorted characteristics of your original family, including such elements as family roles, rules, interactional structures, and behavioral patterns.

This book is a guide for those who desire to probe the contours of their own personal uniqueness. The information and exercises contained in the following chapters are based on the assumption that you discover yourself when you explore your family of origin. As you work through the material, you will develop a deeper understanding of the nature of families. You will discern why your original family functioned the way it did. Also, you will discover the unconscious elements of the script you are now living, a script that often masquerades as your real self. Once the unconscious elements become conscious, you can choose whether to continue with that particular script, modify it, or write a new one altogether.

References

Fagan, J., and I. L. Shepherd, eds. (1970) *Gestalt Therapy Now*. New York: Harper & Row.

Jourard, S. M. (1964) *The Transparent Self*. Princeton, NJ: D. Van Nostrand Co.

Keen, S., and A. Valley-Fox (1989) *Your Mythic Journey*. Los Angeles: Jeremy P. Tarcher.

1

Systems and Individuals

When you look at your hand, what do you see? There is a cluster of fingers, each with its own size and position. There is also a palm to which all the fingers are connected. Your hand may appear to be a collection of different parts, yet this is an illusion. Your hand is much more than a blend of five fingers and a palm. As Ronald W. Richardson mentioned in *Family Ties That Bind*, your hand functions as a whole. Each finger on the hand develops its own "personality" in relation to the rest of the hand. The fingers and palm each function in their own particular way for the hand to be a hand. If one finger is lost for some reason, the entire hand is affected and can no longer function as it did before the loss. Each finger accommodates to the loss and functions in a slightly different way. In this sense, your hand works as a system—an interconnecting network of separate working parts. The individual parts influence the functioning of the hand, and the functioning of the hand shapes the performance of each individual part.

What can be said about your hand is also true of your body. Your physical being is a network of several diverse systems, each with its own function. There is, for example, a nervous system, a cardiovascular system, a gastrointestinal system, a musculature system, a reproductive system, a respiratory system, and a circulatory system. Activity in all these various systems is broken down into smaller discrete functions. This activity regulates your body's internal processes. These processes require a high degree of organization between the systems in order for the simplest activity to occur in the proper sequence. With this organization operational, your body functions as a whole entity, yet simultaneously this whole entity is composed of the several diverse systems working together in an integrated manner. When one system, or part of a system, dysfunctions, your entire body is affected. This, in turn, prompts adjustments in the operation of your other systems.

In a much simpler fashion, ancient philosophers made the same observation. Using a body metaphor that was current in the first century, Paul, a leader in the early Christian movement, used the systemic functioning of the human body to teach Corinthian Christians how they should relate to one another in the church:

> For the body is not one part, but many. If the foot says, "Since I am not a hand, I am not part of the body," that does not make it any less a part of the body. If the ear says, "Since I am not an eye, I am not part of the body," that does not make it any less a part of the body. If the entire body was just an eye, how would it hear? If the whole body was simply an ear, how would it smell? But as it now is, God has integrated the various parts into one body as he wanted them to be. If all the parts were a single organ, there would be no body. As it is, there are many parts, but only one body. The eye cannot say to the hand, "I don't need you," or the hand to the feet, "I don't need you." On the contrary, even those parts of the body that seem to be more fragile are necessary for the body to function, and the parts of the body that we belittle have a very high value. The parts that appear to be unnecessary need special attention as being essential. The parts that are

recognized as essential do not need this special attention. Their value is already acknowledged. God has perfectly shaped the body, assigning great value to its apparently inferior parts, so that there is no division. All the parts work in harmony with each other. If one part suffers, the whole body suffers. If one part functions well, the whole body benefits. (I Corinthians 12:14-26, my translation)

Paul did not intend these words to be a scientific comment on human anatomy. He lived in a prescientific age and casually used the body metaphor to illustrate how Christians are to behave. Nevertheless, his metaphor demonstrates the interlocking nature of bodily functions. The body cannot operate as a unit when some parts are missing or don't function. This assumes that the body is more than a collection of random parts. The functioning of each separate part affects the body as a whole, and the body as a whole has an impact on the way the separate parts function. This is how a system works.

The Family Is a System

Several decades ago, families were viewed as collections of individuals. A particular family was perceived as including a specific number of persons. Each person was regarded as an individual with his or her own unique existence, apart from anyone else in the family. Attention was focused on the separateness of the individuals. Very little consideration was given to the emotional connection between individuals or the reciprocal nature of their interactions. Since the 1950s, however, families have increasingly been perceived as systems similar to other natural systems. From this perspective, individuals are seen to exist in an inseparable network with other people. Their attitudes, perceptions, feelings, decisions, behaviors, emotional development, and physical health are related to what occurs in their interactions with significant others. This way of observing families is called systems theory.

Systems theory views the family as the primary structure in which individuals are formed and function (W. Nichols, 1988). The main focus is on the way family members operate as a unit. In this regard, systems theory concentrates on *how* families function as they do, rather than *why* they function that way. Individuals are viewed as being subordinate to the family unit, and their behavior is explained within the context of the larger family system.

The systems approach broadens the traditional way of conceptualizing human behavior. That approach, popularized by Sigmund Freud, deemphasized interactions between people and focused on the process within people. Systems theory, conversely, accentuates what happens between persons and deemphasizes what goes on within them. Studying families from this angle, it is apparent that the functioning of individuals—including psychological and physical operations, as well as behavior—is regulated by relationships far more than has been previously recognized (Kerr and Bowen, 1988). Systems theory thus is concerned with family organization, family roles, family behavioral patterns, and family communication structures (Friedman, 1985). From a systems perspective, the functioning of particular family members, to some degree, is shaped by the family unit. How individuals behave is understood and assessed in terms of their functioning within the total family matrix, rather than as persons separate from the family group.

Systems are defined in various ways. They have been described as a set of elements standing in interaction (Von Bertalanffy, 1968). Nichols and Everett (1986) defined a system as a complex of interacting elements and the relationships that organize them. Gregory Bateson explained a system as a unit with a feedback structure which processes information (1987). More simply, a system refers to an entity composed so that the whole is affected by its several parts, and the parts are affected by the whole.

Virginia Satir compared the family system to a mobile (1988). All objects attached to a mobile are in balance with each other. When a tug is exerted at one point, tension is communicated over the whole mobile and every part moves in reaction to the tension. The same phenomenon happens in families. When the family is stressed at one point, the stress affects the whole family. Individual reactions to the stress, in turn, influence how other family members react. This triggers a circular process wherein each person responds to the other's reaction.

Three weeks ago, Kim observed that John, her husband, was becoming increasingly distant in their relationship. When they are together, John does not behave in his typically spontaneous and attentive manner. He doesn't talk as much as usual, and seems to be preoccupied with other matters. Although John is actually struggling with a problem at the office which he doesn't wish to discuss, Kim assumes that his distancing is evidence that he is losing interest in their marriage—a presumption that escalates her anxiety. As a result, Kim can't sleep, concentrate on her work, or even finish a meal. She repeatedly badgers John to talk about the issue during their evening hours together at home, but John resists the pressure to talk and gets extremely irritated by Kim's barrage of questions. He expresses his anger in brief, caustic remarks before withdrawing into a brooding silence, a tactic that heightens Kim's anxiety even more, convincing her that he really has lost interest in the marriage. In turn, this galvanizes Kim's desire to question John even more intensely. Unable to settle the issue with John, Kim spends hours venting her fears to her younger sister, who lives with them. The sister sides with Kim, and snubs John when he is around out of loyalty to Kim. John, unaware that he has done anything to offend his sister-in-law, feels hurt by her rejection and withdraws even more. This process continues day after day. Kim, John, and Kim's sister are trapped in a chronic impasse that none of them knows how to resolve.

If you analyze the example closely, you will notice several features about this particular family's interaction:

- No one's behavior stands alone. Everyone's reaction is in response to someone else's action.

- Each person's behavior is understandable only within the context of the other's behavior.

- What affects one individual in some way affects all individuals.

- The question of cause and effect is inadequate to explain these interactions. This question is like asking, "Which came first, the chicken or the egg?"

- Each person's behavior is part of a larger pattern of family functioning.

When you observe the total family pattern, instead of focusing on the behavior of one individual or one segment of the circular interactions, you are viewing the family from a systems perspective.

Characteristics of the Family Systems Model

A systems perspective involves a new way of observing reality. Rather than viewing an entity in terms of cause and effect, as well as individual functioning, a systems perspective focuses on wholeness, interaction, and circularity. Consider the following as examples of systemic thinking:

The viewer and that which is viewed are two parts of a larger totality. Robert is hiking in the mountains. At a certain vantage point on his walk, he stops to admire the majestic view that unfolds before him. The mountains and valleys extend before him as far as he can see. Robert acknowledges to himself that the scenery is breathtaking. According to traditional thinking, he separates himself from the scenery. He is a separate individual viewing the scenery that is before him. From a systems perspective, however, Robert is part of the scenery.

When you contrast yourself with the material world, you are likely to assume that you are separate from whatever is there. You are especially inclined to think this way if you conceive of your body as a separator. This is a common assumption. Many people believe themselves to be encased in a body that separates them from everything else. From a systems perspective, however, your body is a joiner, not a separator. It joins you to the world. Your senses join you to what is happening "out there." Your nostrils, lungs, and circulatory system connect you to necessary oxygen. Your feet link you to the ground on which you move. People die whenever they are completely separated from the world and its environment. In actuality, there is a critical and necessary symbiotic relationship between individuals and the world that perpetuates the continuation of life. Your body joins you to this process. Perceiving yourself as being inseparably related to, and dependent upon, the natural world is systems thinking.

Entities seem to exist separately; but, in reality, nothing exists solely by itself. Everything is inseparably related to something else, and achieves its identity from that relationship. Think about a red apple for a moment. The outside is covered by a thin, red skin. The inside is composed of white pulp. In order to penetrate the inside of the apple, you use a knife to cut the apple in half. Now you've exposed the inside, right? Wrong. Now you see the outside that's inside. Cutting the apple does not uncover the inside of the apple. It merely changes the apple's appearance, all of which happens to remain on the outside. After the cut, half the apple's outside is red and half is white. You can cut all you want, desiring to arrive at the inside of the apple, but the dissecting never works. You keep getting outsides. The inside and outside of an apple always exist together. You can never separate them.

Or imagine you are looking at a basket. You see the outside of the basket and want to view the inside. So, you look over the rim and peer down at the basket's interior. From this angle, you see the inside, right? Wrong again. You are looking at the outside that's inside. The surface on the inside of the basket is no different from that on the outside. Both inside and outside are all of one piece. In this particular instance, the outside just happens to be on the inside.

In the same fashion, all human experience exists in polarity with something else. Nothing has an existence entirely separate from all else. Every up has a down. Every fast has a slow. Every in has an out. Every good has a bad. Seeing polarities as a whole, rather than breaking them down into discrete parts, is synonymous with systems thinking.

According to systems thinking, entities interact with each other in circular patterns, rather than in linear cause and effect fashion. One entity will respond to the stimulus of another, and the other will react to the response of the first. This circular pattern maintains and regulates the interconnection of the several entities. If you have ever watched a basketball game, you have observed this circular process. A player with the ball moves one way, stimulating the defensive player to respond. The defensive player's response will instantly trigger a countermove from the offensive player. This player's action sparks an impromptu reaction from the defensive player. While these two players interact with each other, all the other players on both teams are doing the same thing. The action of the players is circular in nature. Each player continuously reacts to the other's reaction, and so forth. Consequently, each player's performance is intelligible only within the context of the play of everyone else. This is characteristic of systemic relationships

In systems thinking, there is a special focus on wholeness. This implies a necessary reciprocal relationship between all parts of the system. Consider Chopin's *Prelude No. 4*. Lovers of classical music often thrill to this masterpiece. Their tendency is to focus on the individual notes. In reality, though, the silent pauses between the notes are just as necessary for the melody. Without the silent pauses, the notes would be one undifferentiated musical mass. There would be no melody or theme. And what is true of *Prelude No. 4* is true of every piece and type of music. The sounded notes combine with the silent pauses to create the music. One aspect does not exist without the other.

Systems thinking always considers the interplay and interconnection of related entitles. An incident reported by several writers illustrates this point (Lederer and Jackson, 1968; Weiner-Davis, 1992). Some decades ago in Canada, observers discovered a mystery regarding the population of rabbits and foxes. Several scientists noticed that the rabbit population had declined significantly. At first, these scientists thought the decrease due to illness, but no disease could be identified. A few years later, scientists were surprised by an inexplicable increase in the rabbit population. The mystery was compounded a short time later by another decrease in that population. This enigma became more intriguing when observers discovered that the fox population was fluctuating in a similar fashion. A report on this phenomenon of rabbit and fox populations was published and, by coincidence, another scientist read the report and solved the mystery. He noticed that, as the number of rabbits diminished, the number of foxes increased. And in the same manner, when the fox population decreased, the rabbit population grew. This scientist surmised that the increased number of rabbits provided a larger food supply for the foxes, which resulted in a greater number of foxes. As the larger number of foxes ate the rabbits, their food supply diminished, which ultimately meant that the fox population declined as well. When the fox count diminished, the rabbit population grew, creating a new food supply for the foxes. This was a self-perpetuating cycle. The interrelated fluctuations in the rabbit and fox populations provide a model of systems thinking. The increase and decrease in numbers of rabbits made no sense when studied in isolation. The same was true for the numbers of foxes. Yet when both were observed as two aspects of the same natural cycle, both became understandable.

For several decades, systems theory has been applied to families, enhancing the base of knowledge about how families work. Investigating families as systems, which operate like other natural systems, enables researchers to discover what makes families functional and dysfunctional. The systems viewpoint also reduces the preoccupation with the individual, expanding our focus to the entire family unit.

Learning to observe families from a systems perspective isn't easy. It's probably foreign to the way you've been taught to think, especially with respect to linear cause and effect. The following concepts define the general characteristics of systems, and may help adjust your perspective to this particular way of thinking about families.

Wholeness. Families are more than a collection of individuals who are essentially detached from one another. A family system has wholeness (Nichols and Everett, 1986). This means that each member is emotionally attached to every other member. No one is absolutely independent. What influences one member affects all members in some way. A change in one member's functioning will trigger a shift in the functioning of other members. Based on this observation, a systems perspective focuses on behavioral patterns within the family unit. The emphasis is not on *why* an individual behaves a certain way, but rather on *how* a particular behavior relates to the behavior of others in the family. A single behavior is unintelligible by itself. It is meaningful only when interpreted within the family as a whole. In family systems theory, specific behaviors are best understood within the total family system.

The concept of wholeness is demonstrated by Dave's experience. Dave is 51 years old. He enjoyed a very close relationship with his father while he was alive. They regularly talked on the phone, frequently met each other for dinner, and occasionally attended football games together. After Dave's father died of cancer, Dave attempted to fill the void by developing a closer relationship with his youngest child, a son who closely resembled Dave's father.

His new closeness with his son affected Dave's family in several ways. His wife, Betty, became jealous of his closer ties with their son, especially when she noticed that Dave distanced a bit more in their own relationship. Consequently, Betty became more remote from the 16-year-old boy and increasingly hostile toward Dave. In response to his mother's aloofness and his father's expectation that they do more things together, the son began to resent having less time for his own friends, but he did not express these feelings to either parent. Out of loyalty to his father, the son stopped doing things with his friends and began spending more time around the house. Simultaneously, his two sisters got angry with their father because he neglected them. They also became jealous of his closer relationship with their brother. This triggered numerous conflicts between the two sisters and their brother.

You will notice from this example that every person in the family was influenced when Dave established a closer relationship with his son. Everyone was affected because a family system possesses wholeness. Although persons in a family are emotionally connected to one another, what affects one touches everyone. The attitudes, feelings, perceptions, and behaviors of individual members are constantly stimulated by what is going on in the family unit.

Nonsummativity. In 1958, Adolph Rupp, coach of the Kentucky Wildcats, won his third NCAA basketball tournament. The team that won this championship was not made up of particularly talented players. In fact, the five starters were so average in ability they were called the "Fiddlin' Five." This label came from their coach, who remarked, "Those boys certainly are not concert violinists, but they sure can fiddle." During each game of the basketball season, the players appeared to "fiddle around" on the court. They didn't always look or play like championship players. Yet they finished the season as the best team in the nation. The "Fiddlin' Five" illustrates the concept of *nonsummativity*.

Nonsummativity simply means that a certain entity is more than the sum of its parts (Nichols, 1988). Each of the "Fiddlin' Five" starters was an average player. No one of them was especially talented. If someone could have devised a way to combine the talent of these five players, their aggregate abilities would still have been "average"; and 1958 would have translated into a mediocre season. But that is not what happened. What the team demonstrated on the basketball court added up to much more than ordinary performance. There was an indefinable something created by the interaction between these players that transformed "average" into "excellent." Together, the "Fiddlin' Five" produced a unit that comprised far more than the sum of its individual members.

Nonsummativity also can be demonstrated by baking a cake. The recipe for your favorite cake probably calls for ingredients like sugar, flour, butter, eggs, flavoring, and the like. All of these are mixed together and baked at a particular temperature for a specific time. What results from this concoction is far more than the ingredients themselves. The final product doesn't even resemble any one of the ingredients. The cake itself is something more than the sum of its various parts. It is not contained in any of the separate ingredients, but evolves from the interaction between the various ingredients and the heat. What comes out of the oven is more than what goes in.

Families are more than the sum of the abilities, talents, characteristics, potentialities, behaviors, and uniqueness of each individual member. Summing up the parts does not provide the total picture. The reason is that all the members continually interact in some fashion. This interaction produces new and unexpected situations, alliances, desires, reactions, behaviors, feelings, perceptions, and functioning patterns. Consequently, a family is best understood only when these phenomena are viewed within the context of the family system. A family is always more than the sum total of its members. This is one reason why a family is not just a collection of individuals.

The concept of nonsummativity is illustrated by the crisis described below:

> The Jackson family is comprised of a mother, father, and one son. For the past two months, Joan, the mother, has been spending weekdays caring for her aged mother, who is recovering from a serious bout with rheumatoid arthritis. Joan's husband and son care for themselves while Joan is away. When she is at home on weekends, she is too exhausted to do many of the caretaking tasks she normally does, and is emotionally unavailable to the family.

> Responding to his mother's absence from the home, the 11-year-old son, Jake, begins to misbehave at school, and refuses to do his homework and household chores. Jake's father is irritated by his son's behavior, and feels overburdened by his additional caretaking responsibilities during the week. Dad frequently vents his rage toward Jake, which results in numerous hostile confrontations between the two.

> Hoping to find a peaceful respite from the stress-

filled week caring for her mother, Joan returns home on weekends to a highly charged atmosphere. She responds to the situation by feeling angry with both her husband and son for what she considers to be a lack of sensitivity to her dilemma, as well as their inability to cope better with the crisis. Joan handles her anger in her usual passive style by saying nothing. Yet, during the week, she unconsciously expresses her frustration through sarcastic remarks to her mother. Picking up on Joan's irritation, and supposing that it's in reaction to her disability, Joan's mother becomes increasingly agitated, which in turn exacerbates her arthritic condition.

The Jackson family is more than the sum of two parents, a son, and a grandmother. As the vignette demonstrates, family interactions can stimulate emotional reactions and behaviors that would not exist otherwise. The interactions between the four members of the Jackson family influenced the health, emotions, and behavior of each individual. Jake's dysfunctional behavior is unintelligible apart from his mother's absence and father's rage. Dad's rage makes sense only in the context of the whole family situation. Joan's response to everyone is triggered by her circumstances at home, as well as her caretaking responsibilities to her mother. And even though Joan's mother did not know any details about what was happening in her daughter's household, those unknown events had the power to worsen her own arthritic condition. The interaction of individuals in the Jackson family created elements that would not have existed if these individuals were effectively isolated from one another.

What is true for the Jackson family is characteristic of all families. The interaction of family members creates more complexity than would exist if those members were not part of the family. At any given point in time, a family is always more than the sum of its various parts.

Equifinality. Robert and Sue are a brother and sister who grew up in an autocratic family. During childhood, they were not permitted the freedom to develop their own individuality. Their father kept his family on a tight rein. He told everyone what to do and when and how to do it. He was not affectionate, nor was he supportive. Robert and Sue both tried to win Dad's approval in childhood and adolescence, but found it impossible. It was awful for them being objects of their father's anger and reprimands about never amounting to much. They also resented their mother for never interceding on their behalf with their dad. Over time, each offspring developed an alternative style for dealing with Dad. Sue became very passive. She was frightened of her father's wrath and learned to mask all her feelings and opinions. She attempted to control his rage by complying with whatever he said. Robert, on the other hand, was more combative. He became very aggressive whenever his dad had one of his outbursts. He verbally attacked his father and blamed him for being rigid and insensitive. This resulted in numerous conflicts between the two. These conflicts became more intense as Robert reached his late teens. Now in their mid-twenties, Robert and Sue are establishing their own families and have only infrequent contact with their parents. Nevertheless, both have carried into adulthood the coping styles they learned in childhood. Sue continues to be passive and Robert is still very aggressive.

Have you ever wondered how children can grow up in the same family and develop personal coping styles that are so vastly different? This phenomenon is not unusual. Families often produce individuals with widely differing personalities and behavioral styles. This occurrence is explained by a concept called *equifinality*.

Equifinality means that the same results can be secured by starting from different points and using various means (Nichols, 1988). Another way of putting this is that different outcomes can originate from the same activating event (Figure 1). The opposite is also true. The same occurrence can result from different activating events (Figure 2). The first phenomenon is illustrated by Robert and Sue, mentioned above. Robert's aggressiveness and Sue's passivity both resulted from a reaction to their dad's authoritarian parenting style. Casey and Ir-

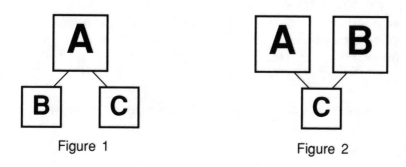

Figure 1   Figure 2

ving illustrate the second concept—that diverse activating events can produce the same result. Both of these men were raised in single-parent families. Casey's mother was overprotective. She constantly monitored her son's activity. When Casey felt the urge to climb a tree, his mom stopped him, explaining that he might fall and hurt himself. Whenever Casey attempted to do some difficult task, Mom stepped in and helped, saying that he couldn't do it by himself. Every time Casey turned around, it seemed that his mother was there to shield him from some supposed danger or failure. Consequently, Casey developed an extreme case of low self-esteem. He believed that his mom rescued and protected him because he was incapable of doing anything by himself.

Irving had a different experience in childhood. His mother seldom reacted to anything he did. In fact, she was rarely around when he needed her. She never encouraged or consoled him when he failed at some venture, nor was she very approving when he succeeded. His mother was totally absorbed in her own career and left Irving to parent himself. Irving interpreted her distance as evidence that he was unlovable and unimportant. His interpretation translated into low self-esteem.

Although Casey and Irving had mothers with different parenting styles, both men developed low self-esteem. This illustrates one dimension of equifinality which affirms that diverse activating events can produce a single result. Both aspects of equifinality define a process that occurs in every family.

Feedback. Families are regulated by a circular feedback system that is similar to the workings of a household thermostat. Once activated, the thermostat mechanism operates by a feedback structure that governs the surrounding atmosphere. When the room temperature drops to a certain level, the thermostat signals the furnace to supply more hot air. When this raises the room temperature to a designated level, the thermostat shuts off the furnace. This triggers an automatic process wherein the temperature affects the thermostat and the thermostat influences the temperature. This reciprocal interaction constitutes a circular feedback system (L'Abate, Ganahl, and Hansen, 1986).

Family process functions in a manner similar to the thermostat. Each family member responds emotionally, intellectually, and behaviorally to perceived input from other family members. This response, in turn, triggers an emotional, intellectual, or behavioral reaction from other family members. Their reaction elicits another response from the first member, and the feedback continues in circular fashion. In family interactions, members continually react to each other's reactions.

This circular tendency is illustrated by one of Sam and Cissy's behavioral patterns. Sam and Cissy have been married for 11 years. Over the course of their relationship, they've developed a particular way of dissolving conflicts without addressing the real problem. Since snags in their relationship are seldom addressed or resolved, both Sam and Cissy now easily get frustrated and angry with each other. Their behavioral pattern goes like this:

- Cissy will complain about something Sam is doing.

- Sam hears the complaint and responds only with a gloomy expression.

- Cissy observes his expression and confesses that she may not be stating the complaint correctly.

- Sam assures Cissy that she is not the problem. He is a failure.

- Cissy counters that Sam is not a failure. She's the one who has blown the whole incident out of proportion.

This process continues until both Sam and Cissy tire of the exchange and establish closure by dropping the whole matter. Their relationship limps along until another problem arises. Then Sam and Cissy replay the same pattern all over again.

The circular feedback network that regulates family relationships is apparent in the experience of Sam and Cissy. One will pick up cues from the other's words, tone of voice, facial expressions, and body language. These stimulate a reaction. The other notices the reaction as it is signaled through words, tone of voice, facial expressions, and body language. These cues elicit another response that is reflected in words, tone, facial expressions, and body language. The cycle repeats itself until one of the partners quits the game. This type of feedback regulates all interactions in a family. No one behavior or emotional response stands alone. Everything is a reaction to another's action.

Homeostasis. The human body is a self-regulating system that maintains a steady state in the presence of changes in the environment. The baseline temperature of your body, for instance, is 98.6 degrees. Despite outside temperature, various regulating mechanisms—such as perspiration, change in water retention, shivering, and "goose pimples"—are activated to maintain your body temperature at 98.6. This tendency of the body to maintain balance, or equilibrium, is called *homeostasis*.

From a systems perspective, homeostasis refers to the internal interactional processes that help maintain family balance whenever that balance is disrupted (Nichols, 1988; L'Abate, Ganahl, and Hansen, 1986). Suppose that the Johnson family is in a state of equilibrium. The family is functioning in a normal, balanced manner. Suddenly, the tranquil household is disrupted by two quarreling children. The kids' anxieties are heightened by their increasing hostilities. Yet it doesn't end there. Mom's and Dad's anxiety also escalates as the two children get louder and more violent. The family unit has lost homeostasis. Increasing anxiety caused by the sibling argument has upset the normal balance of the unit. Responding to this situation, either Mom or Dad is likely to intervene with one or more techniques to defuse the problem. This might include a tactic such as sending both children to their rooms, lecturing one or both, hugging both and encouraging them to settle the argument peacefully, or punishing one or both for their behavior. There is a wide range of techniques the parents might use. Whatever their choice, the goal of parental intervention is the same: returning the family to its previous state of balance. Families have a natural and automatic tendency to restore a state of equilibrium whenever that state has been disrupted. This tendency is called homeostasis.

Devices that families use to maintain equilibrium are called homeostatic mechanisms. The automatic character of these mechanisms is demonstrated by the Alexander family. One Saturday afternoon, the entire family was enjoying an outing in a local park. A loud and terrible cry from one of the children impelled Mom and Dad from their lawn chairs. Their five-year-old son had stumbled over an obstacle and hit his head on a rock. The child lay unconscious on the ground. The anxiety and concern of every family member accelerated.

This crisis immediately upset the family's equilibrium. Automatically, Dad knelt over his son to care for his needs. On a word from her husband, Mom raced to the nearest public telephone to call the emergency squad. The two other siblings hovered close to their brother and consoled each other that he would be okay.

The homeostatic mechanisms in this episode include:

• Attending to the injured son

• Obtaining outside help

• Providing mutual reassurance

All these behaviors were instinctive reactions to the sudden crisis, automatic and instantaneous. Of course, they were also intended to alleviate the trauma that threatened the young boy. Such behaviors served to resolve the crisis and return the family to its baseline state of equilibrium.

Family balance varies from system to system. The Smith family, for instance, has a tradition of verbalizing anger. Whenever there is a conflict, family members freely vent whatever they feel. Anyone is welcome to enter the battle. The Smiths, however, do have a boundary. People can shout but are not allowed to engage in physical violence. Loudness does not unbalance the normal family state, but physical aggression does. The Jones family, on the other hand, handles conflict a bit differently. Members of this family do not raise their voices during an argument. As long as family members use quiet voices, the family remains balanced. If anyone speaks in a loud or hateful manner, however, the family equilibrium is upset.

Every family has its own particular level of equilibrium. Within a particular family system, a range of behaviors and events will be considered normal and acceptable. The system tolerates the anxiety produced by events and behaviors that remain within the accepted range, thereby maintaining homeostasis. Behavior or events, however, that deviate from the accepted range will escalate anxiety to a level at which the family loses its equilibrium. At this point, the family unit will employ homeostatic mechanisms to reestablish balance (Goldenberg and Goldenberg, 1985).

In a manner similar to that of the human body, family homeostasis is a self-regulating force: it helps families maintain a steady state in the presence of significant internal and external pressures and function effectively in stressful situations.

Subsystems. The Duke basketball team won the national championship for the second year in a row in 1992. Throughout the NCAA tournament, TV commentators praised the Duke "system," a program designed to produce excellence in the classroom as well as on the basketball court. Although most of the media hoopla focused on the players and the coach, the Duke system includes a number of other persons. There are assistant coaches, trainers, student managers, physicians, statisticians, teachers, tutors, and the like. All of these people comprise the system, while each individual or group of individuals involved constitutes *subsystems*.

Every system, including the nuclear family, is composed of these smaller units called subsystems. Each subsystem has its own functions, rules, and responsibilities that affect the larger system. The functioning of the human body provides a metaphor. If you conceive of the whole body as a system, the total unit is dependent on several self-regulating and interlocking subsystems. These subsystems include the nervous system, the cardiovascular system, the gastrointestinal system, the respiratory system, the reproductive system, the muscular system, and the circulatory system. The functioning of each separate subsystem and the interaction between subsystems determine how the body itself functions.

An individual is the smallest reducible subsystem within the larger system of the nuclear family. Husband and wife form a spousal subsystem. The children constitute another subsystem. A parent and one or more children make up the parent-child subsystem. All family members of the same sex (mother and daughters or father and sons) compose gender subsystems. Each of these particular subsystems has its own role and responsibilities within the total family unit, and influences the functioning of the whole system.

The concept of family subsystems can also cross generational lines. If one perceives the extended family as a system, the nuclear family can be seen as a subsystem. In similar fashion, a community can be viewed as a system. In this case, subsystems would include extended families, nuclear families, and all the subsystems that compose the nuclear family. If you reason further, a state can be perceived as a system. Its subsystems would include communities, extended families, nuclear families, and subsystems of single families. The concept of subsystem can ultimately be used to understand the entire human race as a system. And the issue doesn't end there. Considering the human race, as well as other animate and inanimate systems, the entire earth can be explained as one whole and interconnected ecological system.

Exercises

Fully understanding yourself apart from your family system would be like fully understanding this sentence apart from the context of the whole paragraph. It simply can't be done. You make sense as a person only within the context of your family system. The following exercises are designed to help you integrate systems thinking into the way you perceive yourself.

Visualization:
Broadening Your Perspective

After reading this paragraph, lay down the book, close your eyes, breathe deeply for a few moments, and visualize this scene. You are hiking through an unfamiliar forest, probing territory where there is no path to lead you. You are exploring on your own, pioneering through a maze of trees and thick groundcover. As you move through this uncharted terrain, notice the trees, listen to the sounds of nature, and observe the various types of plant life that carpet your way. At a certain place in your journey, the trees and undergrowth become so dense you cannot see clearly which way to go. You become disoriented and lose your bearings. You're lost. Now imagine that a huge hot-air balloon appears out of nowhere and gently whisks you high into the sky. As you slowly rise above the treetops, your perspective on where you are begins to change. Your view broadens, revealing the direction you should travel. Stop now and imagine this scene for yourself.

As the hot-air balloon carried you higher and higher, what did you see? Was your perspective transformed? As you drifted higher, did you see valleys and peaks obscured by the dense forest where you were lost? Did distant horizons come into view? With your longer perspective, did you gain some definite bearings as to which way you should travel.

As long as you were focused on the isolated location where you lost your way, direction, bearing, and position were impossible to determine. You remained lost, not knowing which way to go. You were part of the landscape. Yet, as your viewpoint expanded to include the surrounding countryside, your sense of direction and perspective became clearer and more accurate.

Visualizing your ascent in the hot-air balloon is another way of seeing how a part of something always makes more sense when viewed in context. To confirm this truth, pick up any magazine or photograph that's handy. Tuck your index finger under your thumb to form a small circle, and pretend the circle is the lens of the camera. Place the lens anywhere on the picture or magazine cover you've selected. What do you see? A few colors or shapes? Now slowly open the lens until it includes the whole picture.

What you originally saw inside the small circle makes more sense when viewed in context. A part of something is always more meaningful when viewed in relationship to the whole. This principle is as true for people as it is for the visual world.

If you imagine yourself as the only figure seen through a lens, your perspective will be narrow and limited. You will see yourself only as an individual without points of reference or comparison. If the lens is opened to include your whole family in the picture, what happens to your view of yourself? Do you make more sense as a person in this context? Can you see possibilities for change?

Identifying Family Characteristics

In a family system, everyone is emotionally connected to everyone else. What affects one person in the family affects every other family member in some way. You can begin identifying how this process worked in your own family by drawing a map that highlights the major characteristics of each family member, beginning with yourself. This is a model of how the process works:

1. Ray is a 29-year-old pharmacist who characterizes himself as shy, reserved, and a loner. He is uncomfortable in social situations and has few close friends. If you look at him in isolation from his family, this is all you see—a shy, reserved, and lonely person. His figure on the family map would look like this:

Ray

Ray admits that he is dissatisfied with his life. He believes that he locked into the shy, reserved, and loner mode because that's the way he's made. Looking at him in isolation from his family, you might agree that he is simply and naturally shy. Yet, if you observe Ray within the context of his family, you'll see something quite different.

2. Ray's father was distant, unaffectionate, and, at the same time, invasive. He failed to respect his son's personal and physical boundaries. He frequently opened Ray's mail, snooped in his room, and listened in on Ray's phone calls. Early on in childhood, Ray would attempt to draw close to his father, only to be rebuffed or ignored. Ray's mother was unaffectionate, critical, and controlling. She was forever pressuring Ray to dress in a manner that pleased her, to have the friends she wanted him to have, and to behave in a manner consistent with her expectations. Her approval of Ray was conditional upon his compliance with her rigid demands. Mom's and Dad's figures on the family map look like this:

Dad   Mom

3. When Ray is viewed within the context of his original family, his characteristic shyness, reserve, and solitude begin to make more sense. In response to his father's confusing message of distance and

invasiveness, Ray's aloofness shielded him from the emotional pain of rejection, and preserved a measure of his privacy. In response to his mother's efforts to control him, Ray's aloofness protected him from being smothered, and simultaneously enabled him to maintain his own unique identity. As a child, Ray unconsciously protected himself by adopting these coping behaviors and habits. The more his father invaded his privacy, the more reclusive Ray would be. The more reclusive he was, the more persistently invasive his Dad would be. The more Ray's mother tried to control him, the more he would shy away. The more he withdrew, resisting her control, the more his mother would dictate and criticize. Through the ebb and flow of the family's interactions, Ray and his parents encouraged and reinforced each other's characteristic behaviors.

4. Within this broader family perspective, Ray's personality characteristics take on a greater significance. Seen as an isolated indivi-

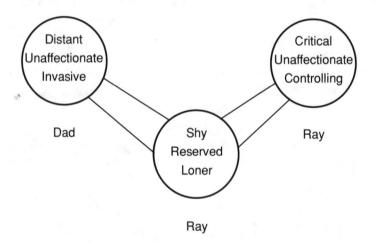

Ray

dual, Ray appears merely to be shy, reserved, and a loner. But in light of his family system, the shyness looks more like prudence, his reserve can be seen as an expression of vigilance, and his bent for solitude clearly seems the result of a very natural desire for independence. Ray did not come into the world as a shy and reserved loner. He crafted these qualities as adaptive skills, enabling him to survive in his family. Over time, Ray rehearsed these skills so often that he confused them with his immutable identity, and lost sight of his capacity for change.

With the model of Ray and his family as a guide, chart and evaluate your own most salient personality characteristics using the four-step process outlined below. As you do so, remember that

- The primary purpose of this exercise is not to determine why you are the way you are, but rather the goal is to identify how you mutually interacted with members of your family.

- You don't need to blame family members for your characteristic behaviors. You simply want to achieve a broader understanding of them.

- The overall purpose of this exercise is to enable you to begin evaluating yourself from a systems, rather than a purely individualistic, perspective. As you complete the assignment, don't be concerned about whether your perceptions are consistent with reality. Even if your perceptions of yourself or your family members are not completely accurate, they are still the "reality" to which you respond.

Step 1: Viewing yourself. On a separate sheet of paper, draw a circle that represents yourself. Inside the circle, list the main three or four traits that characterize you as a person. When you've finished listing the traits, reflect upon being this kind of person in isolation from everyone else. Relate the traits to memories from childhood and circumstances in your present life. Evaluate each trait as to whether it helps or hinders you in living the life you really want to live.

Step 2: Mapping your family. Draw a circle representing each member of your original family. Inside each member's circle, list the major characteristics of that person as you perceive him or her to be.

Step 3: Identify interactions. Using the information you've written down, recall the ways in which family members manifested their characteristic traits when interacting with one another. Focus on your own actions and reactions within the family. Write notes on how your characteristic behaviors were triggered and reinforced by other family members' actions, as well as how their reactions were reinforced by what you did.

Step 4: Reinterpret your traits. As you view yourself within the context of your family, what new perceptions come to mind? Do you begin to see that your characteristic traits evolved as a reaction to others in your family? From this broader perspective, do the characteristics you listed for yourself in Step 1 emerge in a new light? Do you see a new significance from them? Complete your evaluation by noting specifically how a family perspective has altered your perception of yourself.

Summary

This chapter examined some of the characteristics of family systems. Special focus was given to the concepts of wholeness, nonsummativity, equifinality, feedback, homeostasis, and subsystems. Some of the major points were as follows:

1. Families are understood best when viewed from a systems perspective.

2. A systems perspective focuses on the functioning of the whole family, rather than on isolated behaviors of individual members.

3. The attitudes, emotional responses, and behavioral patterns of individuals are intelligible in context of the entire family unit.

4. In families, every person is emotionally connected to everyone else. Whatever has an impact on the family affects each member. And whatever has an impact on each member affects the whole family unit.

5. At any given point in time, families are more than the sum of their individual parts. The interaction between family members creates something that doesn't exist apart from that interaction.

6. In families, identical results can be triggered by diverse activating events. Also, the same activating event can stimulate different results.

7. A circular feedback process operates in families. In part, this means that each person constantly reacts to everyone else's reactions.

8. All family systems have a natural tendency toward homeostasis. Whenever the unit is unbalanced by any kind of stress, homeostatic mechanisms automatically kick in to restore equilibrium.

9. The family system is always composed of subsystems. The individual member is the smallest irreducible subsystem in a family unit.

References

Bateson, G. (1987) *Steps to an Ecology of Mind.* Northvale, NJ: Jason Aronson.

Friedman, E. H. (1985) *Generation to Generation.* New York: The Guilford Press.

Goldenberg, I., and H. Goldenberg (1991) *Family Therapy: An Overview.* Monterey, CA: Brooks/Cole Publishing Co.

Kerr, M. E., and M. Bowen (1988) *Family Evaluation.* New York: W.W. Norton & Co.

L'Abate, L., G. Ganahl, and J. C. Hansen (1986) *Methods of Family Therapy.* Englewood Cliffs, NJ: Prentice-Hall.

Lederer, W. J., and D. Jackson (1968) *The Mirages of Marriage.* New York: W.W. Norton & Co.

Nichols, W. C. (1988) *Marital Therapy.* New York: The Guilford Press.

Nichols. W. C., and C. A. Everett (1986) *Systemic Family Therapy.* New York: The Guilford Press.

Richardson, R. W. (1987) *Family Ties That Bind.* Vancouver: International Self-Counsel Press Ltd.

Satir, V. (1988) *The New Peoplemaking.* Mountain View, CA: Science and Behavior Books.

Von Bertalanffy, L. (1968) *General Systems Theory.* New York: Braziller.

Weiner-Davis, M. (1992) *Divorce Busting.* New York: Summit Books.

2

Family Roles

When you watch a movie or a play, can you distinguish the actors from their roles? Because actors infuse a part of themselves in the characters they portray, do you ever confuse the role with the actor? In the classic film, *The Old Man and the Sea*, Spencer Tracy plays an old fisherman. In reality, Spencer Tracy is not that fisherman. He only plays the part. In another exemplary film, *Zorba the Greek*, Anthony Quinn plays the lovable Greek, Zorba. Of course Anthony Quinn is not really Zorba. He has an identity of his own and only impersonates that character in the film. The audience knows that an actor is not really the person portrayed in any particular play or film. Actors are not the people they impersonate on stage. They have an identity of their own.

In some ways, families are like plays. They have a script that they follow and embellish over time. And families have a cast of characters, each with a specific role that is fashioned according to the rules of the script. Unlike the roles that actors play, however, family characters and roles are not always consciously recognized for what they are. Actors are aware of their role in a play, and they consciously perform the role according to the script. They generally do not confuse the script with their own life. This is not true of family roles and scripts. Individuals may not be aware that they are playing a particular role in the family, and they often confuse the role with who they really are. This happens because family roles and scripts mostly operate at an unconscious level.

There are many people around who groan their way through life, despising both the script they live and the role they play. These people are inclined to be unhappy and frustrated with life. Usually they believe that things will never change—that they must remain forever the way they are. Limited by this belief, they endure roles that no longer fit and are extremely uncomfortable. They laboriously follow a script that lacks meaning and interest for them. These people are destined to live out lives that are unfulfilled and incomplete. They are susceptible to a wide range of physical, emotional, and spiritual disorders. They are doomed to unhappiness and discontent.

Such individual live lives of desperation because of a delusion. They confuse scripts and roles with themselves. They are like an actor who tires of his role in a play, but continues the engagement, becoming more and more despondent. Such people come to believe that they are really the roles they impersonate.

Can you make the distinction for yourself that you make with actors in a play? Can you distinguish yourself from your role? Or do you confuse your role with the real you? As long as you scramble the two, you will unconsciously perpetuate the role, believing that this is the way you really are.

It's actually possible to distinguish yourself from the script you follow and the role you play. Both of these originated in your childhood. From the day you were born, you were assigned a particular role in your family system. Over time, you unconsciously identified yourself with the role, and it became second nature to you. By exploring your original family, you can identify the unconscious role you play, bringing it to a conscious level. Once this occurs, you are free to change the role any way you please. You can retain portions of the role you want to perpetuate and scrap those you dislike. Or you can replace the role altogether. Life roles and scripts are not immutable. They can be changed and rewritten. Yet, before this happens, you must discover what they are. Then you can be like an actor who discards a monotonous role in a dull play for a role in a new play that offers more stimulation and meaning.

Family Goals

Every family is organized to meet certain goals. These goals are family objectives, such as caring for the physical, spiritual, and emotional needs of family members, supplying such necessities as clothes, food, and a place to live, and providing an education for the kids. Goals like these influence how a family is organized, as well as how it functions. For this reason, identifying the goals of a family partially explains why families work the way they do. This is because parents structure and supervise their family so that goals can be achieved.

Family goals can be described in various ways. They can be long- or short-term. A long-term goal involves a distant future accomplishment, like providing a college education for each child, or assuring an adequate retirement for Mom and Dad. A short-term goal targets an achievement in the near future, like accumulating enough cash for a summer vacation, saving for a down-payment on a new car, or stashing away money for next Christmas. Most families, in some fashion, have both long-term and short-term goals, even when these are not clearly defined.

Family goals can be formally set or merely implied. Parents in one family, for instance, determine that their kids will get summer jobs when they're old enough, and go to college after high school. These expectations are openly communicated to the children from a young age. The parents in another family, on the other hand, may not discuss particular goals for their children, either with each other or the kids. These parents merely assume that the kids will work outside the home when they're old enough, or will attend college. When goals are assumed or implied, rather than openly and clearly expressed, there is a higher risk for confusion, conflict, and dissatisfaction within the family.

Family goals can also be differentiated in terms of their primary or secondary nature. Families vary as to goal priorities, yet all families have a priority schedule. In some families, material objectives are primary, while intangibles are secondary. In such families, a six-figure salary may be more important than time spent with each other; or buying a particular house may get more attention than adequately communicating with a seven-year-old. Other families, however, place intangibles, such as pride, happiness, or personal fulfillment, above material objectives. Parents always set priorities for their goals according to what they consider important. For this reason, goals reveal something about a family's values.

There are also conscious and unconscious goals in families. A conscious goal is one that spouses talk about or that is implicitly agreed upon. In either case, the spouses are aware of these goals. An unconscious goal is one that motivates family functioning, but is unrecognized by family members.

The difference between conscious and unconscious goals is demonstrated by Alice and Donald. Alice was the oldest of four children in her original family. As the oldest, she frequently functioned as a surrogate parent for the three youngest kids. By the time she reached young adulthood, Alice was an accomplished caretaker. Donald, on the other hand, was the youngest of two kids. As the baby of his family, he was accustomed to having others make a fuss over him and take care of his needs.

When they became engaged, Donald and Alice had good reasons for getting married. They were conscious of being in love, and both agreed that they wanted to share their lives with each other and raise a family. Neither, however, was aware of an unconscious purpose in their relationship. The unconscious agreement in their marital contract called for Alice to take care of Donald. Because this goal was unconscious, the two never discussed or recognized it, yet its existence permitted both to carry on with the roles they learned in childhood. Consequently, whenever Alice failed to do something Donald expected or wanted, he became very angry and critical of her behavior. Over time, Alice came to believe that Donald was inconsiderate and controlling. Donald began to view Alice as selfish and insensitive. These perceptions had a negative impact on their marriage, but neither understood what was happening. Both were unaware that their behavior was motivated by an unconscious agreement. Donald and Alice's experience is not unique. All marriages and families have both conscious and unconscious goals, contracts, and expectations.

Goals vary among families. Yet whatever their aims happen to be, all families organize and structure themselves to achieve both their stated and unstated goals. This is accomplished by setting rules, allocating responsibilities, and assigning individual roles to each family member. These individual roles are especially vital for the family. In addition to helping the family achieve its goals, the roles played by individuals determine how the family functions as a unit. They also govern each family member's development.

Functional Roles

Every family develops various behavioral patterns for its members. These patterns are called *roles*. The roles prescribe who does what in the family, and enable the family to function effectively on a daily basis. There are two types of roles, *functional* and *systemic*. Each type has its own repertoire of expected behaviors.

Primary Functional Roles

Functional roles are consciously assigned in the family and empower it to operate efficiently as a unit. The primary functional roles include husband, wife, father, mother, and child. Although there is some similarity between family groups, the expected behaviors for each of these roles vary from family to family. In the Calhoun family, for example, the husband and father is responsible for earning a living outside the home. Additionally, he is responsible for house maintenance, lawn and gardening tasks, upkeep of the family cars, and supplemental caretaking of the kids. The wife and mother in this family views her outside job as auxiliary to her husband's, while her primary task is running the household and serving as major caretaker for the kids. The kids, in this system, have no assigned or regular responsibilities. They are merely expected to obey family rules and do whatever their parents ask.

In contrast to the Calhouns, the Brown family has a different set of expected behaviors for primary functional roles. Both spouses consider their careers equally vital to the family's well-being. They share household tasks, as well as parenting responsibilities. Their children are given regular duties around the house, such as cleaning their own rooms, and are expected to comply with parental rules.

Whether openly expressed or merely assumed, roles in every family are accompanied by a group of expected behaviors and responsibilities. These behaviors and responsibilities enable the family to meet the needs of its individual members and achieve collective goals.

Secondary Functional Roles

The secondary functional roles involve specific tasks that are necessary for the smooth running of the family. These include being cook, maid, grass cutter, maintenance person, family chauffeur, dishwasher, laundry worker, timekeeper, appointment maker, recreation manager, spiritual director, family nurse, disciplinarian, and mechanic. Every task that needs to be done in the family is assigned to someone's role. In a theatrical performance, all goes smoothly when the cast plays its roles according to the script. This is also true for families. Whenever family members perform their roles properly, the family functions efficiently and people are more likely to get their needs met. Whenever family members perform poorly, or ignore their roles altogether, the family flounders, personal needs remain unmet, and family goals are not achieved.

Systemic Roles

Families also assign *systemic roles* to individual members. These roles are called systemic because they preserve the uniqueness of the family system. Like their functional counterparts, systemic roles comprise a repertoire of expected behaviors. Unlike functional roles, however, systemic roles are unconsciously assigned to particular family members. Because these roles are unconscious, they significantly influence the individual's personality development. It is not uncommon for families to equate a member's role with his or her own unique personality. For this reason, people tend to perpetuate their particular roles long after they have reached adulthood and left their original family.

The systemic roles mentioned most often by contemporary writers include *caretaker, family hero, scapegoat, mascot,* and *lost child* (Wegscheider, 1981; Whitfield, 1991; Kitchens, 1991). All families, to a certain extent, develop such roles, although the particular roles themselves, as well as their composition, may vary from family to family.

In more flexible families, roles occasionally may be exchanged among family members. The lost child, for instance, might function as the caretaker, the family hero may assume the role of mascot, or the scapegoat may grab a few moments in the sun as hero. Families with a more rigid structure permit very little role exchange. In these families, individuals function only in their assigned role. The caretaker is always the caretaker, the hero is always the hero, the scapegoat is always the scapegoat, the lost child is always the lost child, and the mascot is always the mascot.

In either flexible or rigid family systems, it is not uncommon for one member to play several roles, or for two members to be assigned the same role. The latter is more common in large families. The former is typical of small families. Charles L. Whitfield, in *Co-Dependence: Healing the Human Condition*, categorizes the various family roles according to four patterns. The *classical pattern* involves a person who plays only one role. The *sequential pattern* describes a person who shifts from one role to another. A *mixed pattern* designates individuals who simultaneously play more than one role. A *non-classical pattern* refers to any combination of roles that varies from the first three patterns (Whitfield, 1991).

The Caretaker

The family caretaker, as the name implies, cares for the needs of family members. This role frequently is assigned to the wife/ mother, with one or more children designated as caretaker-in-training. Caretakers perform a multitude of tasks which can include anything from preparing meals to bandaging a skinned knee. Their tasks commonly include making doctor and dental appointments for family members, chauffeuring the kids to soccer games or music lessons, picking up dirty clothes left on the floor, reminding other family members about upcoming birthdays, listening to groans about how awful life is, and working as peacemaker for two feuding members of the family. There is no end to what caretakers do for others in the family.

In dysfunctional families, caretakers often become *enablers*. If a family member has an addiction, or some other type of disorder, caretakers often enable that person to maintain their dysfunctional behavior. Enablers do this by assuming responsibility for the other person's problem and attempting to control the dysfunctional behavior. Since this is usually an impossible task, enabling caretakers generally end up feeling helpless, fearful, frustrated, and angry.

Enabling caretakers also tend to overfunction in the family. They do for others what others should do for themselves. Over time, those playing this role become vulnerable to various physical illnesses, as well as numerous emotional and spiritual disorders.

Carrie illustrates how caretakers can overfunction. She has been married for 19 years and has three children. For the past three years, she increasingly has become dissatisfied with life, secretly wishing she had the courage to walk off, leaving everyone and everything behind. That wish, however, is only a fantasy. Carrie continues to plod through each day doing what she has always done. In addition to a part-time job outside the home, Carrie prepares all the meals for her family. She cleans the house alone, makes all the beds every morning, and picks up after everyone, as well as being responsible for cutting the grass. On Sundays, she lays out the clothes for her husband and three teenagers. She even ties her husband's tie. After church, Dad and the boys change clothes and leave their suits crumpled on the floor, but Carrie hangs them up so that they won't be wrinkled for next Sunday's use. Although she tires of doing all these chores, Carrie is mostly frustrated and hurt by the insensitivity of others in the family. They seldom offer to help, express appreciation for what she does, or even recognize that Carrie herself has needs that are not being met. Over time, Carrie has become extremely dissatisfied with her roles as wife and mother. That's why she now fantasizes about leaving her husband. And that is why she's receiving treatment for depression and anxiety attacks.

On the surface, it appears that Carrie's husband and teenagers are the villains in this scene. This appearance, however, is only an illusion. Carrie and her family are involved in a cooperative and circular behavioral pattern. Carrie overfunctions for other family members. Those members collude with Carrie by underfunctioning. They invite her to overfunction, and Carrie enables them to underfunction.

Carrie may or may not be typical of caretakers in other families, yet she demonstrates several occupational hazards of this role:

- Caretakers tend to overfunction for others

- Caretakers place family needs above their own

- The needs of caretakers usually are ignored by other family members

- Caretakers neglect their emotional and physical well-being in favor of caring for others

- Caretakers disguise weakness with a mask of perpetual strength

- Caretakers, over time, experience frustration, fatigue, and chronic anger

- Caretakers feel selfish when they consider doing something for themselves

The Hero

The family *hero* is responsible for making the family look good in the community and creating pride among individual family members. Children who are assigned this role are typically overachievers in school, as well as superresponsible in church and community activities. Family heroes are people-pleasers who get attention and approval by doing what adults expect. They attempt to be perfect, and feel good about themselves only when they live up to the expectations of others.

As adults, family heroes perpetuate overachieving behaviors. They are successful at work, assume leadership roles in church and community, and become superresponsible in relationships. Adult heroes believe that they need to be perfect, and they gain their self-esteem by giving others what they need, as well as by providing for their own family.

The perils of being a family hero include:

- Neglecting one's own needs and ambitions in order to fulfill the expectations of others

- Becoming addicted to behaviors that please others

- Feeling extremely guilty when pursuing one's own desires

- Feeling loved only when pleasing others

- Being overly dependent on others for feelings of self-worth

- Vulnerability to guilt and depression when failing at some task

- A tendency to develop stress-related disorders

The Scapegoat

The role of family scapegoat is opposite to that of hero. The member designated as scapegoat acts out the family's problems. This role can be assigned to anyone in the family, but usually is given to one of the children. The selected child often becomes defiant and hostile, and struggles with behavior problems. In the absence of positive affirmation or approval, the scapegoat gets attention by misbehaving. By accepting blame for anything from being undependable to having a character disorder, this child deflects attention from other difficulties in the family. The rest of the family members can ignore or deny their own problems by focusing on the scapegoat. As family dysfunction increases, the scapegoat will intensify his or her problem behavior.

When scapegoats become adults, they are likely to repeat their cycle of misdeeds. They may abuse alcohol and drugs, or develop some other compulsive behavior that perpetuates their image as a loser. Such people may become irresponsible adults who thrive on negative attention. It is not uncommon, however, for some adult scapegoats to transform their negative childhood conduct into hard-nosed competitive behaviors, becoming successful in business or other careers. Whether one perpetuates the scapegoat role in adulthood or transforms that role into more productive behaviors depends on such variables as role rigidity in the original family, the degree of role blending and dysfunctionality there, and the level of emotional damage resulting from childhood. If, for instance, a person in a mildly dysfunctional family plays a blended role of scapegoat-hero in childhood, she might direct her compulsiveness toward more acceptable hero behaviors in adulthood.

The liabilities of the scapegoat role include:

- Low self-esteem

- A tendency to repeat self-defeating behaviors in adulthood

- A vulnerability to chemical abuse or other unhealthy compulsions

- A profound sense of guilt and shame at the core of one's being

- A tendency to become antisocial

- A proclivity for being preoccupied with oneself

- An inclination to accept blame for anything that goes wrong

- A belief that, no matter what one does, one can never really amount to much

The Lost Child

The lost child role calls for one to cope with the family system by avoiding all that's going on. The child selected for this position learns to withdraw from any conflicts or emotional chaos in the family. This is accomplished by physically leaving the scene. The lost child spends a considerable amount of time in his or her room, or playing outside. When this is not an option, he or she copes with family distress by emotionally shutting down, a process that includes dissociating from one's feelings. The lost child usually is mild-mannered, obedient, and a high achiever. Children in this role are unlikely to do anything that draws attention to themselves. They merely do what is expected and attempt to stay out of the way of other family members.

In adulthood, the lost child normally remains quiet, mild-mannered, and inconspicuous. Such adults perform their tasks well with very little fanfare. They avoid conflict situations, and seldom express strong emotions. Frequently, they exhibit a high degree of independence, and are sometimes accused of being aloof. Even as an adult, the lost child will tend to shut off emotions in a crisis.

Lost children are exposed to several risks, including:

- A diminished ability to enjoy the fullness of life

- A limited access to their emotions

- A heightened feeling of loneliness

- A tendency to run away from painful situations

- A sense of being unloved and unappreciated

- A sensation of being unattached and isolated

- Low self-esteem

- A hesitancy to express emotions, disagree with others, or ask for what they want

The Mascot

The function of the mascot is to provide relief and comfort for the family. This need is created whenever stress threatens to unbalance the family system. On these occasions, problems and difficulties are defused by the mascot through comic routines. He or she is the family clown, the one who makes everyone laugh. Although the conduct may not always be humorous, the mascot role requires one to entertain or annoy other family members with a wide range of antics and cute behaviors. Sometimes the mascot is valued as a clown. On other occasions, the mascot is scorned as a pest.

Family mascots grow into adults who continue getting attention by entertaining others. They are experts at defusing stressful situations with humor or some other distracting behavior. Some are able to pull this off with finesse. They relate well to others, are comfortable in social groups, and make everyone in the office, or all the guests at a party, feel more at ease. Other mascots, however, fail at the role of adult comic. Their attempts at humor come off as put-downs or otherwise offensive behavior.

The hazards of being designated the family mascot include:

- A difficulty taking one's self seriously

- A tendency to mask one's emotional pain and anger with humor

- A diminished ability to express one's real feelings

- A hesitancy to disagree openly with others

- An inability to ask for help or for what one needs

- An inordinate sense of responsibility for how others feel

- A lack of skill at confronting stressful situations

- A need to be the center of attention

- A highly developed ability to placate others

As you assess the different roles used in your family system, try to keep several general observations in mind:

- The roles used in any particular family will be determined by the needs, goals, values, and inner dynamics of that family.

- Not all the roles defined above will necessarily be played out in any given family.

- Each family creates roles with the family's own distinctive imprint. The descriptions given above may not correspond exactly to roles in your own family.

- An individual family member may have a role that is a composite of one or more of the roles described above.

- One person in a family sometimes plays several roles.

- People who grow up in dysfunctional families are more likely to use their role as a lifelong coping mechanism. As adults, they will repeat role behaviors in any situation that is similar to those experienced as a child.

- Individuals tend to confuse their personality with the roles they played as children. For this reason, childhood roles are frequently replayed throughout adulthood.

In addition to the major systemic roles, there are also a number of supporting roles. These include behaviors that may be adopted from time to time by anyone in the family, regardless of his or her major role. These supporting roles are similar to major roles in that the more rigidly they are followed, the more they characterize your typical behavior and tend to be mistaken for your real personality. Some common supporting roles are described below.

The martyr. This part calls for self-pity, feeling unappreciated or misunderstood, and reminding others of all you do for them. Martyrs try to control and manipulate others by using guilt and feigning helplessness.

The perfectionist. This part involves fear of failure or of making any mistakes. The requirements of the role demand that you be driven by a compulsive need to succeed and overachieve.

The persecutor. The persecutor is one who verbally attacks or demeans another in the family.

The rescuer. The rescuer attempts to liberate or protect the family member attacked by the persecutor.

The abuser. This role calls for one family member to violate another, either physically, emotionally, verbally, or sexually.

The victim. This is the person who is the object of the persecutor, abuser, or bully.

The dunce. This part calls for one to feign ignorance or inadequacy. The family dunce will excel at failing or botching simple tasks. Dunces are expected to make blunders, and often live up to that expectation.

The bully. It is usually insecure family members who assume the role of the bully. They attempt to control situations by lashing out at others or verbally threatening them.

The odd person out. The odd person out is unattached from the family unit. He or she seldom joins in family occasions, and is frequently not even informed about family activities.

The critic. This role is played by one who claims to know everything and scorns advice. The critic is never wrong about anything, and is quick to criticize other family members, pointing out their failures and flaws.

The guru. The guru is the keeper of the family's cache of oral tradition which has accumulated over the years. This includes the clan's wisdom, history, and customs. The role of guru is usually played by a parent or grandparent, but it can be the responsibility of any older member of the extended family. The guru passes on to younger family members the exploits of their ancestors, both near and distant. The guru's stories and teachings reflect the family's traditions and values. These stories overtly or covertly delineate what it means to be a member of this particular clan. Statements such as, "The Fosters do it this way," or "A Cohen never lies!" are common guru expressions.

The little angel. This is the person who always maintains his or her innocence, even when having instigated some mischief among other family members. The angel does nice things for selected family members, and always strives to appear saintly. Often, the angel is designated as a favorite child by one of his or her parents.

Identifying Your Family's Cast of Characters

The material on family roles will enhance your understanding of yourself when you apply it to your own family. Use the list below to identify who played the various roles in your original family, and whether the person continues the role in adulthood. As you assign the cast of characters in your family, remember that not every family has players for all the roles. Some families have roles that are not included in this list, and family members often play more than one role.

Family Role	Family Member	Role Continues (yes or no)
Caretaker		
Hero		
Scapegoat		
Lost Child		
Mascot		
Martyr		
Perfectionist		
Persecutor		
Rescuer		
Abuser		
Victim		
Dunce		

Bully	_____	_____
Odd Person Out	_____	_____
Guru	_____	_____
Critic	_____	_____
Angel	_____	_____
Other	_____	_____

Family Roles and Personality

The word _personality_ comes from the Latin _personare_. This is a compound word made of _per_ and _sonare_, meaning "to sound through." Originally, this word described ancient Roman and Greek actors, who wore a mask for each character they portrayed in a play. As an actor changed from one role to another, he would don a new mask. According to Greek custom, it was considered sacrilegious for actors to perform barefaced. They always had to wear the specially designed character masks. These masks all had very large openings for the mouth, enabling actors to project their voice so that everyone in the amphitheater could hear them. The actors would literally "speak through—_personare_—the masks.

Since the ancient theater masks were fashioned to reveal the character of whatever god, person, or animal was being re-created on stage, the word _personare_ came to be used for the habitual traits that characterized each person in a play. In time, the word, "personality" came to designate an individual's habitual features which are usually displayed in interactions with others. Your personality, in this sense, refers to a repertoire of behaviors and traits that normally characterize how you react to others and life in general. Even though you may consider your normal responses to be "just the way you are," this assessment may not be entirely correct. A certain portion of your personality is neither the way you are nor the way you have to be. It is merely the way you _learned_ to be, acting out a script imprinted on your unconscious mind.

The roles assigned to you in childhood, as well as the flexibility or rigidity with which these roles were regulated, had a profound impact on your personality development. However you describe yourself as a person, the way you characteristically behave now is a composite of the ways you learned to behave in your original family. Your normal behavior—how you interact with other persons, how you respond to particular situations, how you manage your emotions, as well as coping styles you've selected—is influenced by the role or roles you played as a child. Over time, these roles became comfortable and enabled you to get through life with a minimum of emotional distress. As an adult, you are likely to continue the same roles, either consciously or unconsciously, although your present circumstances may be far different from those that prevailed during your childhood.

Betty's experience exemplifies how family roles crafted in childhood are repeated in adulthood. Betty was 56 when she realized that her life was going nowhere. The youngest of her four children left home three years before, the same year that she divorced her alcoholic husband. Although Betty had a responsible position as a nurse, she was haunted every day by a deep sense of emptiness and guilt.

Betty grew up in a large family, the only girl among five boys. When she was seven, her mother underwent the first of numerous hospitalizations for mental illness. With Mom out of the home, Betty was pressed into service as a surrogate mother. She prepared the meals for her father and brothers, did the wash, cleaned the house, and performed all the tasks her mother was unable to do. She functioned in this role until she left for college.

This experience in her family of origin groomed Betty to be a caretaker. She found meaning in taking care of others. The extent to which she was shaped by this role was demonstrated by the man she chose to marry, as well as the career she chose to follow. Both involved caretaking.

Toward the end of college, Betty was involved with two different men who were interested in marrying her. One of them, Bill, was self-confident and a go-getter. He had a promising future in business. Tom, the other man, was talented and ambitious as well, but he was not nearly so self-confident and assured. He was beset by insecurities rooted in his childhood. Betty chose to marry Tom because, in her words, "He needed me more than Bill." Her decision was prompted by her caretaking role. She needed someone who needed her.

Over time, Tom became an alcoholic. Betty cared for him, raised their four kids, and worked as a nurse for almost 30 years. After the kids left home, and Tom's drinking problem got worse, she decided to leave the marriage. Following her divorce, Betty felt a sense of freedom for a short while. The freedom, however, was soon replaced by feelings of emptiness and guilt. The emptiness was spawned by the fact that Betty no longer had anyone to care for. Caretaker was the only role she was trained to play. Having no one who needed her translated into a deep sense of meaningless.

Betty's struggle with guilt was triggered by the same situation. As a good caretaker, she felt solely responsible for the marriage. Her failure to solve the problems that ruined the relationship with Tom evolved into guilt. Betty was haunted by thoughts that the marriage would still be intact if she had been a better caretaker. In her mind, she was responsible for Tom's drinking and his refusal to do anything about it. Her guilt was built into the caretaking role.

Ted was given the role of hero in his family of origin. He was the child unconsciously designated by his parents to make the family proud and enhance the family's image in the community. His grades and participation in athletics and in civic activities produced compliments from everyone in the community. His role called for him always to behave appropriately, be an overachiever, be successful, and make other family members feel good. His parents, siblings, and extended family all looked up to him. In their eyes, Ted could do no wrong. He was destined for greatness.

Early on in childhood, Ted began internalizing the high expectations verbalized by his parents. By the time he reached late adolescence, he was highly driven by these internal standards. He felt worthless whenever he failed to attain the expectations first set by his parents.

Both consciously and unconsciously, Ted pressured himself to please his family by overachieving, continuing the hero role after leaving home. He graduated from college at the head of his class, finished medical school, married a young woman approved by his parents, and settled in his home town. Over time, Ted became a model husband, an exemplary parent, a respected physician, and a leader in his church. The hero role seemed to pay big dividends as his personal reputation flourished and his medical practice prospered, but that was not the whole story. Ted was slowly creating the circumstances for his own downfall.

At first, Ted didn't notice how much stress was caused by the internal messages that drove him toward increasingly higher levels of success. As his reputation grew, the scope of his heroism encompassed a larger crowd, including his original family, his own wife and child, his patients, medical colleagues, and fellow members of his church. He pressured himself to achieve more and more, and scrupulously monitored his thoughts and behaviors lest he let someone down.

Ted's fragile world began crumbling during his wife's second pregnancy. Although he didn't understand why, he began feeling more and more distant from her. He rationalized this as a passing phase, and ignored the stress on their marital relationship until he realized that he was emotionally attached to his secretary. This realization created a serious crisis in Ted's marriage. After months of agonizing struggle and futile attempts to repair the damaged relationship, Ted decided to leave his wife. The consequences of this decision were as momentous as he feared. There was an immediate outpouring of censure from his wife, friends, and colleagues. His medical practice suffered, as well as his leadership role in the church. Ted was embarrassed and confused by his extramarital involvement. He was not the kind of person to do something like this. He was a hero, and heroes didn't act this way.

Although Ted struggled and agonized over the impact his separation had on his practice and reputation in the community, his biggest conflict came from disappointing his original family. He was a fallen hero, and that was almost more than he could bear. His parents, brothers, and sisters were mystified. They could not fathom why Ted did this. They became very angry, and pressured him to remain in his marriage. They were primarily concerned about Ted bringing shame on the family. Ted was sent reeling into a cycle of depression and guilt. He ended up taking a leave from his practice and receiving psychiatric help.

Betty and Ted are not unique. There are myriads of people who do not know where their childhood family role ends and their own personhood begins. These individuals confuse their personality with the role they played as a child. In adulthood, that role defines them as a person. It prescribes how they behave, feel, and think in particular situations. Creatures of habit like everyone else, these people tend to perpetuate their roles, even when those roles produce negative results.

This tendency is strengthened by two powerful reinforcers. Family roles are comfortable, having been rehearsed from childhood, and provide individuals with a familiar mode of behavior. Roles are also replicated in adulthood because people mistake the repertoire of behaviors required of a particular role with who they are as a person. When a person plays a role for years, it is not uncommon to believe: *This is just the way I am. I can't change.* Armed with this belief, a person will repeat his or her assigned role without giving it a second thought.

Analyzing Your Roles

This is an exercise to help you evaluate the roles you play in your significant relationships. Use the six columns of the schema to analyze each role and its accompanying goals, behaviors, and characteristics. Detailed instructions follow below.

1. In the Role column, list the main role you play in each of your significant relationships. Document each relationship in a separate row, including your role with each of your parents (if living), your role with your spouse, with each of your present family members, and with each of your close friends.

2. In the Goals column, write down your specific personal goals for each relationship listed. Relate these goals to the particular role you play with this person.

3. In the Behaviors column, list the characteristic behaviors required by each role you play.

4. The Flexibility column is for your assessment of how rigidly you adhere to your roles. Approximate the level of flexibility in your roles on a 1 to 10 scale, with 1 being extremely rigid ("Something I feel compelled to do") and 10 being extremely flexible ("Something I do only if I want to.").

5. The Comfort column is the place to rate how comfortable you are when playing your various roles. Estimate the level of comfort on a 1- to 10-point scale, with 1 being excessively uncomfortable and 10 being extremely comfortable.

6. The Value column is for your assessment of the extent to which a particular role enables you to achieve your stated goals. Use the 1-

Role	Goals	Behaviors	Flexibility	Comfort	Value

to 10-point scale again, with 1 standing for "no help at all," and 10 representing "exceptionally helpful."

Once you've entered your data into the schema, you'll be ready to analyze your current roles. Roles that have a lower score in general are probably liabilities to you. Such roles may be those that you've outgrown, that never suited you, or are otherwise limiting. When a role inhibits your development as a person, or obstructs your life goals, it's healthy to respond by modifying or rejecting the role altogether. Of course, this is a process requiring both courage and tenacity!

Changing a Given Role

The way to modify any role is to change the characteristic behaviors that go with it. This process is neither quick nor easy. If you've identified some changes you want to make, the following suggestions may help.

1. *Visualize the change.* Close your eyes and imagine changing the behaviors that identify you with this particular role. What responses do you envision receiving from the important people in your life? What new role will you choose to adopt? Once you've taken on the behaviors associated with this new role, how do you feel? Compare your response in the visualization to the comfort and value scores you noted on the schema in the earlier exercise. Does this new role make sense for you?

2. *List specific behavioral changes you desire to make.* Targeting specific behaviors is more effective than identifying general ones. "I'll express my feelings when my spouse and I are settling a dispute," is more effective in producing change than, "I'll be a better spouse."

3. *Inform significant others of impending changes.* Remember that your behavior affects everyone in your family. Prepare family members for your role change by telling them what you intend to do and why. Handle any resistance by expressing your own feelings, opinions, desires, and needs rather than being blaming or argumentative. This means using "I" statements to inform the other person about what you feel, think, desire, perceive, and will or won't do. For example, "I feel unhappy about being the caretaker for every-

one in this family. I want to change things so that my needs for nurturing get met, too." (Rather than, "You've treated me like a slave for 16 years. I've had it with you people!")

4. *Start small and go slow.* When crafting a new role, start out with new behaviors that will be the easiest for you to adopt and the least anxiety-provoking for your significant others. Changing too quickly can threaten relationships you value (even though you may want and need these relationships to change). Going slowly provides the opportunities to strengthen these relationships as you change.

5. *Be patient with yourself and others.* Roles and their accompanying behaviors are changed over months and years, not days and weeks. Give yourself permission to make mistakes and to backslide. Grant significant others the time and freedom to handle your changes in their own individual ways.

6. *Be consistent.* Consistency, not perfection, is the secret of successfully changing any role. Regularly evaluate your progress and recalibrate your direction when necessary. Realize, too, that there are certain relationships that you may lose completely when you change, even though you will have changed for the better. Chances are that such relationships were toxic, anyway. You'll be better off without them.

The schema on the next page has been filled out as an example to show you how it's done. When you understand the process, fill out the blank schema at the beginning of this exercise.

Roles and Mutability

Individuals often play more than one role inside and outside the family drama. As an adult, you *might* repeat the role assigned in your original family in every area of your life; but it would not be unusual for you to play one role in your family, another with your close friends, and yet another at work.

Although a given role can have an overall positive impact on your personality, many roles prove to be both stifling and restrictive, especially as people mature, when their life circumstances shift, or when relationships change. Roles are enlivening when they allow you to express your own uniqueness and respond to life events in a more

Role	Goals	Behaviors	Flexibility	Comfort	Value
Caretaker with husband	• Companionship • Mutual needs met • Intimacy	• Shop for his clothes • Buy his presents for his mother and other members of his family • Pick up after him	3	2	1
Caretaker with 3-year-old son	• Promote his personal growth • Nurture his emotional development	• Read to him • Bathe him • Feed him • Etc.	3	7	10
Hero with mother	• Make Mom proud • Be a responsible daughter • Feel good about myself	• Be involved in community activities • Daily contact with her • Take her shopping	2	2	4

effective manner. Obviously, they are restrictive when they place un-necessary limits on your happiness and success.

Modifying a role when it is time to change is healthy; yet there are many people who acquiesce to lives that are depressing and pallid by assuming that change is impossible. Over time, failing to modify a role that is no longer relevant or useful can contribute to a wide range of emotional, physical, social, and spiritual disorders.

When you confuse who you really are with the role you play, you inhibit your own growth as a person. This is because, in any given role, there are dimensions of yourself that are distorted, ignored, or suppressed. When you limit your perception of yourself to the roles you play, the neglected dimensions of yourself remain undeveloped and you are never able to "get it all together" as a person. This can include ignoring negative, rather than positive, aspects of your inte-grated personality. For instance, a family hero may never allow herself to play the dunce or the lost child, even though there are times when she feels both inadequate and vulnerable. In the long run, such a per-son can be damaged just as much as the family dunce who never allows herself to be successful.

Roles are both mutable and, ultimately, destructible. Unlike your genetic traits, family roles can be altered, adjusted, manipulated, or rejected completely. The critical factor is to know when to modify a role to fit your own maturity level, meet your changing needs, more effectively match your present life circumstances, and enhance your relationships. You can change or exchange a particular role for another merely by changing or refusing to enact the behaviors required of that role. Bear in mind, though, that your fellow players will become high-ly anxious when you make such a change, even if it is a very positive one for you.

Roles and Anxiety

Imagine that you are in a theater viewing a play. As long as each actor delivers his or her lines on cue and does what is written in the script, things run smoothly on stage. But can you visualize what would hap-pen if one of the actors began reciting the lines of someone else, or suddenly began acting a part from another play? There would be chaos on stage and confusion in the audience. Everyone's anxiety would rise, and one or more people would do something to get the recalcitrant actor back into character. Only then would anxiety diminish and equilibrium be restored.

As unlikely as the fulfillment this fantasy might be in a real theater, it happens frequently in families. An individual who is assigned a particular role in the family is expected to play that role. Whenever someone steps out of character and behaves contrary to his or her designated role, anxiety increases in the family, and equilibrium is destroyed. Family members feel shocked, angry, upset, surprised, or even pleased. If the anxiety gets high enough, one or more people in the family will perform a countermove, doing or saying something to force the errant member back into his or her assigned role. When this member gets back in character, anxiety in the family diminishes, and balance is restored to the family system.

The Marshal family shows how families can be unbalanced when someone steps out of character. This extended family included five grown children, all of whom, with one exception, lived within five miles of Mom and Dad Marshal. Jane, the oldest daughter, was groomed for the role of caretaker from childhood. Now, as an adult, Jane played this role in her own family, as well as in her extended family. When Mom Marshal began suffering from a heart disorder, the larger family assumed that Jane would automatically care for her, which she did. Jane daily kept close watch on her mother's health and would take her for periodic appointments with the doctor. The several times when Mom had to be hospitalized, Jane was the one in charge. She transported her mother to the hospital and stayed with her in the evenings. On these occasions, Jane's brothers and sister expressed appropriate concern over their mother's illness, but none of them offered to help Jane with her caretaking responsibilities. The Marshal family expected each member to remain in character, even in a crisis.

On one occasion, Jane was out of town when her mother had to be hospitalized. Betsy, a younger sister who was the family's lost child, assumed Jane's role and took their mom to the hospital. In a more flexible family, this role change would have been acceptable. The Marshal family, however, was rigidly entrenched: Betsy's role change caused a disturbance. The family allowed Betsy to take Mom to the hospital, but they could not tolerate her staying with Mom. The caretaking role was only for Jane. Yet, in spite of numerous protests that she go home, Betsy stayed with her mother for two days. The longer she functioned out of character, the more family members attempted to countermove her back into the lost child role. Mom, frustrated that Betsy would not go home, refused to talk to her. Betsy's brother objected to her stubborn behavior and would not visit their mother as long as Betsy was in the room. When Jane returned from her business trip, she was infuriated with Betsy for remaining at the hospital. She criticized Betsy for upsetting their mother and ordered her to go home.

As Jane resumed the caretaking responsibilities following her trip, Betsy returned home and skipped back into her role as the lost child. Immediately, anxiety in the family diminished and normal relationships were restored. Jane stayed with Mom in the hospital. Betsy and her brothers visited in the evenings, and everyone talked and interacted with each other as though the family hassle had never happened.

Whenever individuals behave out of character, the family unit becomes unbalanced, and the anxiety of other family members escalates. The degree of disruption in the family is directly related to how rigid or flexible the family is regarding role expectation. In families in which members are rigidly expected to remain in character, anxiety accelerates more quickly, and there will be an increasing number of countermoves when individuals step out of character. In families where roles are more flexible, levels of anxiety are lower, and individuals are permitted a wider range of behaviors outside their designated role.

Exercise:
What Happens When Family Members
Fail To Play Their Designated Role

List a characteristic behavior that was expected of you by your parents, a behavior required by the role or roles you played in your family. After listing the expected behavior, remember an occasion when you acted out of role. How did your parents respond to you? What did they specifically say or do to nudge or force you back into your usual role? What feelings did their countermove trigger inside you, and how did you react?

I was expected to _____

_____

I acted out of role when _____

_____

My parents _____

_____

I felt _____

_____

I reacted by _____

_____

After thinking about one particular occasion when you failed to play your designated role, try to remember an occasion when one of your parents acted out of role—preferably an occasion that involved you. What was your immediate emotional reaction? What did you specifically do or say to countermove your parent back into his or her usual role?

I expected my (mom/dad) _____

_____

(He/She) acted out of role when _____

_____

This action triggered feelings of _____

_____

I responded to these feelings by _____

_____

My (mom/dad) reacted by _____

_____

_____

Summary

1. All families, either intentionally or unintentionally, possess a set of prioritized goals. These goals influence how families are organized and shape how they function.

2. In order to attain their goals and function in an acceptable way, families consciously or unconsciously assign roles to each family member.

3. Individuals tend to identify with their assigned role and frequently confuse it with who they really are. Whenever this happens, persons are inclined to continue playing their role throughout adulthood.

4. Roles that are more rigidly followed in childhood are more likely to be replicated in adulthood.

5. Functional roles—such as breadwinner, cook, maid, chauffeur, mechanic, dishwasher, and the like—enable families to run smoothly on a daily basis.

6. Systemic roles reflect and preserve the uniqueness of the family system. The major systemic roles include caretaker, hero, scapegoat, lost child, and mascot. In addition to these major roles, there are supporting parts such as martyr, perfectionist, persecutor, rescuer, abuser, victim, dunce, bully, odd person out, critic, guru, and little angel. Supporting parts may be played by any family member on a given occasion.

7. A repertoire of expected behaviors define individual roles and supporting parts. Anxiety in the family accelerates when a member behaves out of character. The level of anxiety is related to the rigidity of the family. The more rigid a family is regarding role expectation, the higher the anxiety rises when a member does not play his or her assigned role. The more flexible a family is regarding role expectation, the more comfortable they are when a member behaves out of character.

References

Kitchens, J. A. (1991) *Understanding and Treating Codependence.* Englewood Cliffs, NJ: Prentice-Hall.

Wegscheider, S. (1981) *Another Chance: Hope and Health for the Alcoholic Family.* Palo Alto, CA: Science and Behavior Books.

Whitfield, C. L. (1991) *Co-Dependence: Healing the Human Condition.* Deerfield Beach, FL: Health Communications.

3

Individual Scripts

Ginny, a 42-year-old former client, was trapped in a life that was going nowhere fast. She complained of chronic anger, hopelessness, mood swings, conflictual relationships with family members, and depression. In the course of therapy, we addressed issues related to her current life setting, as well as some undetonated emotional landmines from her past which remained buried deep in her unconscious. After recognizing the life script she'd been living since childhood, Ginny remarked with considerable insight, "it's hard to admit that I've been writing my own lines all these years. I sure gave myself a rotten part to play!"

Have you ever wondered who you really are? Beneath the layers of learned behaviors, proper manners, physical appearance, and customary ways of doing things, are you actually yourself, or are you a fabricated self that others want you to be? Soren Kierkegaard, the nineteenth-century philosopher, believed that the deepest human despair results from choosing to be someone other than who you are—

from not choosing to be yourself. At some point in your life, you've probably experienced the anguish of acting a part rather than being who you really are. Perhaps, like Ginny, you've recognized the unnecessary pain you've inflicted on yourself because of this false role.

How do you get the life you live? Who wrote the script you perform and the music to which you dance? Are you free to choose the profile of your existence from an unlimited number of possibilities, or is that profile predetermined by your genetic heritage and environment, with no input from you? Does your human experience have any genuine significance, or is it merely a shadow, having no substance or reality of its own? If you're dissatisfied with the way things are going, are you free to change them? Are you only who you perceive yourself to be, or is there more to you than meets the eye?

Perhaps you've noticed before that the words *quest* and *question* share a common root. A genuine quest always involves questions. For this reason, questions like those above are essential in the quest for yourself. Such questions can help you decipher the cryptic puzzle of personal identity. They probe the enigma of inner space and the mystery of individual human life, enabling you to discern whether you are truly being yourself. Is everyone's destiny written in the stars? Or is there a more down-to-earth reason why people turn out the way they do?

There is no simple or comprehensive answer to such questions about your personal identity and manner of life. This is because you create your life from an intricate blend of circumstances, arbitrary occurrences, genetic imprinting, and personal choices. You have a measure of freedom to define yourself, yet this freedom is limited by certain boundaries over which you have no control. These boundaries include such factors as genetic inheritance, the family system into which you were born, the ethnic group to which you belong, the culture of which you are a part, and the era in which you live. The extent to which these and other factors shape your life is determined by the way you respond to the factors themselves. For however perplexing the questions about life may be, the bottom line is that human beings have an innate ability to mold the character and course of their own lives.

In crafting your individual life, you do not create yourself *ex nihilio*, out of nothing. Rather, you fashion yourself from the tangible and intangible elements that are given to you, beginning at conception and continuing throughout your lifetime. One of the intangible elements that shapes separate lives, and with which you must grapple in giving birth to yourself, is the script that was composed in your original family. This script is closely related to the role you played in your family and, like theatrical texts, the script has a theme—or plot— which governs how you live and what you do. In robotic fashion, people unconsciously behave, think, and feel in ways that are consistent with this script. You do this so routinely in the early years of life that you eventually confuse the way you usually are with the way you have to be. For this reason, your individual script, as much as any other element in your existence, defines the contours and parameters of your life.

Sam Keen, in *Fire in the Belly*, suggests that to be free we must demythologize the authority that has unconsciously shaped our lives (Keen, 1991). Among other things, this means that you must become conscious of the individual myth, or story, that you are living. Everyone throughout time has enacted an individual and unconscious myth that is embedded in every family's history.

As long as your personal myth remains unconscious, you are not free to be yourself. Instead, you are compelled to repeat the myth over and over in your daily life, no matter how miserable that might be. Yet, if you uncover the myth you're living, you can experience an exhilarating freedom, enabling you to distinguish yourself from the intangible script that has governed your mind, feelings, and actions for years. To discover this authentic self, you must first identify your own particular script. That script, or myth, comprises the drama you've been performing since childhood.

Your Script and Your Family

Over the years, I have crafted workaholism into a fine art. My goals, aspirations, and ambitions all revolve around work. In addition to being a college professor, I have a private counselling practice and hold weekend workshops and seminars. During football and basketball seasons, I steal a few hours on weekends to watch games that interest me; but other than these selected moments, Saturdays and Sundays are for research and writing. Until recently, whenever someone commented about my work habits, I usually responded by saying, "That's just the way I am. I'm a workaholic." Now, however, I no longer make that claim, because I know it isn't true.

There was a time, when I was younger, when work wasn't such a consuming passion. I'd take time off to loaf, dawdle, and dally. I enjoyed family outings, and spent hours reading or doing nothing in particular. During my sophomore year in college, I recall taking a minimum number of hours so I'd have more time for tennis. That was not a unique occurrence. It was typical of how things used to be. In my youth, play always got top billing over any kind of work.

As I grew older, the work compulsion got stronger. It particularly began dominating my life about the time my father was diagnosed with terminal cancer. He was able to stretch 18 months, which the doctors gave him, into five years. During those five years, as he became increasingly immobilized by the cancer, I became more activated, transforming hard work into workaholism. At the time, and even several years after his death, I didn't understand what had happened to me. How could a talented dawdler so quickly develop into a compulsive worker?

Now I understand that my workaholism had nothing to do with the real me, but was all part of a family script I instinctively followed. Anticipating my father's death, I began acting on one of his most profound unconscious fears, the fear of being a failure. On closer investigation, I discovered that this hadn't just begun when he started to die; I had been shaped by this script throughout my childhood. This script called for a carefree boy to evolve into a successful man obsessed with work. As long as my script was unconscious, I followed it, because I believed it to be descriptive of the real me; I had no choice about being any other way. Now that my script is no longer unconscious, I feel free to continue in this particular role or to modify it to make my life more meaningful and satisfying.

Why does a family, with the unwitting collusion of its members, create scripts for each individual member? I have a hunch that it has something to do with imprinting individuals to guarantee the survival of the family system. Every individual has been genetically imprinted by his or her parents, which assures the continuation of certain biological traits in each parent. The genetic imprinting of your particular DNA code connects you to an ancestral heritage spanning the history of humankind. In a similar fashion, you have received emotional imprinting from your family, which ensures the survival of values, customs, traditions, and ways of being that have evolved within your family system over generations. This emotional imprinting is a kind of script that you're obliged to follow. It enables your particular system to maintain a basic core of family traits across generations of change. No one fully understands why scripting occurs. People who study such things merely know that it happens. People tend to follow their script, confusing it with the way they really are, as long as they live.

Your personal script, like the role assigned you in your original family, is mostly unconscious. Whenever you reveal the script, two momentous options become possible. You begin to understand why you live the way you do, and you become free to rewrite the script if you choose to do so.

Individual Scripts and Early Family Experiences

Wally is now a busy professional in the mental health field. Although he first expressed interest in this career when he was only 12, the road to his vocation took a circuitous route through several careers, including the ministry. For Wally, the ministry and mental health are twins, especially since both were contained in the family script he was given to work with shortly after his birth.

Wally was born into a middle-class family. His father labored tirelessly to provide for Wally's family. His mother worked outside the home as well as functioning as homemaker and Wally's primary caregiver.

As a child, Wally didn't know that his family contained a virus which had infected his family system for several generations. He did know, however, that his parents, particularly on weekends, when his father drank, engaged in serious arguments which sometimes erupted into physical violence. This cycle of discord profoundly affected Wally's development. From an early age, he did not play far from the house on weekends. He stayed close to home, because he knew that sooner or later his parents would get snared in a dreadful argument. When this happened, Wally stood off-stage until it was time for him to play his part in the drama. When his father's anger escalated into rage, Wally would move between his parents, primarily to protect his mother from physical harm. Wally's presence usually caused Dad to withdraw. At that time, Wally would urge his parents to make up, which they always did. A happy ending was also part of the family script. This process would take several hours, but normally Wally's role as rescuer achieved its intended goal.

By the time he was 12, Wally had perfected the roles of peacemaker and rescuer. One day in school, his teacher asked the students in her class to write a brief paragraph on the vocation each wanted to pursue. That's when Wally discovered he wanted to be a psychiatrist, a career he had never before thought about. Why did this idea pop into his mind on that particular occasion? Was it simply a matter of chance? Even though Wally did not consciously connect his family experience with this career choice, his interest in psychiatry was no coincidence.

Three years later, Wally was actively involved in a small church where he was given large doses of attention from some very caring individuals, especially the minister and several adults who worked with the church youth. By this time, things had settled down at home. His father had made profound changes in his own lifestyle. He was no longer drinking on weekends, nor was he venting the anger he had carried from childhood. Consequently, home was no longer a battlefield that called for Wally to play his peacemaking role. As the family script was rewritten, there was no longer a need for the part of peacemaker or rescuer. This new script required Wally to modify his own role in the drama. He soon committed himself to enter the ministry, which was, like psychiatry, a vocation that would allow him to rescue people.

Following seminary, Wally delighted in ministering to others. In time, though, he tired of the laborious administrative tasks that went with his job. They only diverted him from his first love, which was caring for people who were crippled by personal problems. After struggling with his own inner turmoil for several years, Wally resigned from the church. He entered a graduate program in psychology, and became a psychotherapist. This long, circuitous route, which began early in Wally's childhood, was no haphazard journey. By highlighting the influence of family background on individual psychology, it prepared him to be even more effective in fulfilling his role as someone who rescued people.

On the surface, Wally's understanding of vocation may seem to be a jumble of unrelated events. But at a deeper level, all of his experiences can be seen as different aspects of one interconnecting pattern that evolved out of his childhood. Given the emotional environment of his family, Wally was practically destined to be a rescuer. He assumed that role each time he rescued his mother from his dad's rage. When this function was no longer relevant, Wally revised his rescuer script to encompass other people besides his mother. Again this decision was not arbitrary, but was conceived and nurtured in the bosom of his family. Wally's role as rescuer is part of the script he unconsciously created to survive the vicissitudes of life with his original family.

You might question why Wally chose his particular script as rescuer. He might have opted to follow his father's script and become an abuser himself. Or he might have adopted his mother's script as an abused victim. Or he might have selected another script altogether. What factors influenced his choice of role? Was Wally born with a given character that predisposed him to choose the rescuer script, or was that choice merely a fortunate coincidence, or even a spontaneous event that happened for no reason at all? Was his choice shaped by other factors, such as the continuous interaction of Wally's innate abilities, childhood perceptions, and specific family situations? There are speculations on all sides of this issue; but at this point in our understanding of human development, we simply don't know why anyone chooses a particular script. The most anyone can do is simply to describe how the scripting process works.

Although Wally's particular story is unique, the scripting process he experienced is not at all unusual. In some fashion, the process is the same for everyone. Whatever your own script happens to be, you fashioned it unconsciously to fit the circumstances and events of your original family. It was most likely reinforced later by your personal relationships outside your family, even if the original circumstances that made your role relevant no longer abide. In Wally's case, his attachment to obsolete circumstances—his need to rescue people—had a positive outcome. In other cases, people may be playing out negative roles even after the circumstances that engendered them no longer exist. For such people, uncovering the script can mean liberating themselves from the tyranny of a particular role.

Individual Scripts and Lifestyle

Earlier in this century, Alfred Adler, the father of individual psychology, used the phrase *style of life* to describe what is today called a *life script* (Ansbacher and Ansbacher, 1956). He believed that people's individual styles are formed early, usually in the first five years of life. After this age, a person's style doesn't change very much and is generally reiterated throughout life. Individual style may be characterized by such terms as optimism, pessimism, cynicism, complacency, courageousness, or cowardice. In addition to its dominant character, a person's style is composed of general habits, attitudes, and tendencies. These can be activated by any life experience, such as failure, disappointment, relationships, work habits, personal habits, and reactions to crises or changes.

Consider your own characteristic style of life. How do you usually react to stressful events? Do you automatically focus on the negative aspects and become pessimistic? Do you normally concentrate on positive elements and feel optimistic? Do you tackle problems with self-confidence, convinced that you can handle whatever needs to be done? Or do you cower away in some emotional corner and wait for the storm to pass? How do your friends or relatives expect you to act in any given situation? How do you expect yourself to respond in any given situation? Answering such questions enables you to trace the edges of your adopted lifestyle and come close to identifying the scripts you've created.

Exercise:
How I've Responded to Significant Events

You can begin identifying the particular elements of your own lifestyle by completing this exercise. Using the model below, divide a sheet of paper into four parts. Label the upper-left rectangle "Significant Events," the upper-right rectangle "Expectations of Others," the lower-left rectangle "My Expectations," and the lower-right rectangle "Actual Response."

In the top left, list a personal event (occurring anytime from childhood to the present) that you consider to have been significant in shaping the course of your life, for better or worse. Describe briefly in the upper-right box how particular family members and friends expected you to respond to that event; then write down your own expectations at the time. In the bottom right, note how you actually responded to the event.

Significant Event	Expectations of Others
My Expectations	Actual Response

Use separate sheets of paper to complete this exercise for as many events as seem significant to you. After you've digested what you've written down, write a brief paragraph summarizing how the information characterized you lifestyle. In writing your summary, include adjectives that describe your behavior and attitude—terms such as optimistic, pessimistic, courageous, cowardly, aggressive, stuck, and so on. Ask yourself what general habits, tendencies, and attitudes have predominated in your responses to significant life events. On the next page is an example of a filled-out form.

I guess it's pretty typical of me to be optimistic at first about change—and it's also typical of me to take on more than is really appropriate, out of my desire to be seen as strong and accomplished. When it gets to be too much, I go to the other extreme: everything's horrible and I have to get out.

In addition to the notion of a style of life, Adler theorized that people also adopt a *guiding goal* early in life. Such a goal must be compatible with your lifestyle; it's similar to the theme or plot of a play. As the adjective *guiding* implies, the goal determines the direction of your life. You act out or replay that goal in the way you live. Con-

Significant Event	Expectations of Others
Parents divorced when I was 14 years old.	Mom expected me to be her "best friend," and to take over a lot of the household responsibilities.
My Expectations	Actual Response
I thought that things would be saner and more peaceful when we left Dad—but Mom took on a lot of his behaviors.	I did everything Mom wanted at first, but it just got to be too much after a while and I rebelled. I couldn't wait to leave home!

sequently, the guiding goal either facilitates or hinders healthy adjustments to life. People, for instance, may develop a neurotic lifestyle wherein they dominate others, or exploit people, or habitually exempt themselves from work or responsibility. For instance, if a person adopts domination as a guiding goal, this will color how that person responds to others in any given situation. In a fashion similar to the choice of a life script, the selection of guiding goals usually begins as an unconscious process.

Carol, a 53-year-old grandmother, exemplifies the practical effects of a particular lifestyle and guiding goal. Raised in an authoritarian family, Carol learned early in life to cope with distressing events by adopting an optimistic stance. This included a guiding goal of making others feel good. Even as a child, Carol played the eternal optimist. She cultivated a positive attitude and emotional equilibrium that no disappointment was powerful enough to disrupt. In the face of disturbing events, she learned to deny the pain and focus on the bright side. Each negative situation was only an opportunity to grow stronger. If negative elements of an experience needed to be minimized or rationalized, Carol was up for the job.

Over time, Carol's many friends judged her to be a strong and capable person who would conquer whatever adversity life dished out. She has been optimistic throughout her 53 years. And yet Carol wasn't born that way. There was no optimism gene embedded in her

DNA code. This was merely a style she adopted and reinforced until it co-opted her identity. Carol continues the pattern because she can't imagine behaving any other way.

Life Scripts

The notion of a *life script* is actually a corollary of Adler's idea of life-style. This notion is used primarily by adherents of Transactional Analysis (TA) as a helpful device to understand the nature of one's existence. Although the idea of life scripts is more intricately and technically defined in TA literature, there are some general elements that are similar to my use of this concept, elements that can sharpen your understanding of your own script. According to TA, people develop a script for themselves in childhood (Berne, 1966; Harris, 1967; Stewart and Joines, 1987). This script serves as a life plan to help people survive and thrive in their particular family circumstances. Like theatrical scripts, people's individual scripts include certain themes, plots, and subplots. These are acted out in childhood and continue into adulthood. Patterns of choice and behavior in adulthood are strongly influenced by childhood experience; the script metaphor can be helpful in identifying the source material for the roles people play as adults.

Life Script as Drama

Every life script contains its own beginning, middle, and conclusion. Early on, in infancy, people establish the basic plot. Details are added in later childhood; adolescence is spent revising and polishing the script. As adults, most people are unaware of the script they created as children; yet they continue to guide their lives according to the major themes woven throughout the story. Whatever situations arise in their everyday lives, their responses tend to follow the demands of the particular script they have chosen. This is why people individually experience life as a tragedy, or a comedy, or a high drama, or a soap opera, or a thriller, or an adventure. This is also why some people see themselves as heroes, while others play the villain. People become whatever character is called for in their script.

The Nature of Scripts

You created your particular script in childhood. You did not do this consciously, making decisions the way you do now as an adult. Yet, as a child, you formulated your script as the best way to cope in the world you found yourself born into. Based on your interactions with your parents and other significant people, you formed a general view of what that world was really like. This personalized world view, as well as the feelings generated by contact with your environment, provided the raw material for your script. Verbal and nonverbal messages from your parents reinforced the part you were supposed to play. By the time you finished adolescence, the script was final, assuring that you would usually view the world in the same way, and respond to life in the same manner, from then on.

Brad grew up in a chaotic family. Both his parents were alcoholics and knew very little about parenting. They behaved capriciously and were irresponsible in caring for Brad. Consequently, he viewed the world with suspicion. He believed that people cannot be trusted, and that he would always get hurt in close relationships.

Over time, Brad learned that he was not as vulnerable if he encased himself in an emotional shell and stayed away from people. In this setting, Brad created a script that embodied both his view of the world and his beliefs about people and relationships. Performing this script as a child, Brad formed only surface relationships with his peers. He was cautious with all adults, especially his teachers, and seldom expressed to anyone what he really felt or thought. Although he was very lonely, Brad survived his childhood world with the help of the script he crafted for himself.

Now, in adulthood, nothing has changed for Brad except that he is older and much more cynical. A 32-year-old bachelor with no close friends, he views the world as unpredictable, and continues to believe that people cannot be trusted. As a result, he behaves in ways that keep his acquaintances and co-workers at a safe emotional distance. He continues to feel lonely, but has accepted this condition as his appointed fate in life.

Although Brad doesn't see beyond the limitations of his life script, being lonely is not his only choice, nor are his beliefs about people, relationships, and the world necessarily realistic. Brad experiences life the way he does because of the script he has written and continues to follow.

Scripts and Life Positions

Your individual script is based on one of four basic convictions about yourself and others. These convictions express the value you perceive in others and yourself; they are called *life positions* (Stewart and Joines, 1987). The four convictions are:

- I'm not okay, you're not okay.

- I'm not okay, you're okay.

- I'm okay, you're not okay.

- I'm okay, you're okay.

The first stance—*I'm not okay, you're not okay*—assumes that the world is dangerous and full of despair. This is the position of people who devalue themselves and others. These individuals believe themselves to be unlovable and inadequate. Scripts based on this life position are filled with scenes of rejection, loneliness, hurt, and anguish.

People who weave a script around the *I'm not okay, you're okay* position value others, but depreciate themselves. They assume a one-down stance in relation to others, supposing that the needs, interests, desires, and thoughts of others are more important than their own. Scripts based on this life position have themes of victimization and defeat.

Individuals who adopt the *I'm okay, you're not okay* stance esteem themselves and devalue others. They assume a one-up position in relation to others, presuming their own needs and interests to be more important. At times, these people will do whatever is necessary to get what they want, even if they have to hurt others to do so. Scripts based on this life position call for the protagonist to get his or her own way, but at the cost of alienating others. Consequently, these scripts are filled with scenes of rejecting others, being rejected by others, and aloneness.

The *I'm okay, you're okay* life position assumes that the world is friendly and exciting. Those holding this position like themselves and value their own needs and interests. This attitude is extended to others with whom they interact. Equal value is given to other people's needs and interests. Scripts based on this position include themes of cooperation, acceptance, gratitude, contentment, and companionship.

Identifying Your Script

You live your life according to an unwritten and unconscious script. But how do you go about uncovering that script?

Identifying your own particular script is not an easy task. Beginning where you are now in your own life, it involves tracing themes, intuitions, behavioral patterns, and events that lead back to your childhood and original family. The motifs, ideas, hunches, memories, feelings, and intentions involved are often ambiguous and fragmentary. Sometimes your journey will proceed along paths that turn out to be dead ends. Occasionally you'll discover clues you'd just as soon ignore or deny, especially when you uncover a family secret or wander into the shadowy dimension of your own personality. Periodically, you may misinterpret some of the evidence. Yet, if you are diligent and honest, you can arrive at your destination, discovering the script you began creating for yourself before you could talk, and which you have performed every day since its creation.

The following suggestions can help you on your quest to identify the script that is such a vital part of your identity. The suggestions are cast as questions to stimulate a dialogue which can be extremely helpful in discovering meaning and creating insight. Depending on your preferred style, you can reflect on the questions and their answers, write down your answers on a sheet of paper, or verbalize your answers, speaking to yourself only, to a partner, or even into a tape recorder. Writing or speaking your responses to the questions is a good way to trigger new perceptions about your life experiences.

Which of the four life positions mentioned above is the foundation for your script? Analyze your answer for evidence. For instance, if you think you follow the *I'm okay, you're okay* scenario, is this *universally* true? Do you feel that everyone in your family is okay? Or do you take a one-up position with one or more family members? What about peers and associates? Do you feel superior to any of them?

What about other ethnic groups or nationalities? Do you feel or behave as though you were more important than any other group of people?

Once you have identified your basic life position, think about the ways in which that position shapes your daily behavior, as well as your typical attitude.

Who are your heroes and villains? Are your heroes all generic—such as athletes, humanitarians, celebrities, politicians, and other public figures? Are your heroes people who do things such as helping the unfortunate, succeeding in business, serving in the military, or setting a world record? In your mind, what makes a hero?

Do your villains all fall into a racial or cultural stereotype? Or are they people who do dreadful things, like abusing children, polluting the environment, betraying national secrets, or killing someone? In your mind, what constitutes a "dreadful" act and what makes a villain?

Once you've identified your heroes and villains, what does this reveal about your values, ambitions, and basic position in life? How do your heroes and villains influence your daily behavior, choices, and ideals?

What events keep recurring in your life? Do others generally like you and respect your opinions and abilities? Do you typically get rejected in relationships? Do you usually get what you want? Are you often depressed? Are you mostly optimistic or pessimistic? Do you keep feeling disappointed in people? Do you frequently become hurt or angry because of what others say or do? Examine the patterns of events that keep appearing in your life. How do these patterns help you isolate the major themes or plots in your life script? How do they reinforce the beliefs you have about yourself and life in general?

What were your favorite stories and who were your favorite characters in childhood? How are your favorite characters like yourself? How are the themes in your favorite stories similar to the themes in your own life? What events in your life and traits in yourself mirror your favorite characters and stories? Are there any literary characters and stories that you detest?

Everyone has a shadow side, a part of themselves that they abhor. The shadow includes thoughts, feelings, desires, fantasies, and ambitions that are contrary to the self you approve of and accept. Probe into the murky depths of your shadow. What parts of yourself do you deny, ostracize, or ignore? What is there about you that is scary? What about you is dreadful? Even if you vehemently deny these aspects of yourself, they are nonetheless a part of you. How does your shadow side affect the protagonist in your script? How is your shadow woven into the plots in your personal drama? Or how is your shadow written out of the script?

As you answer these questions, remember that your heroes and villains do not emanate from a void. They ascend from deep within you, shaped by forces at work deep inside your psyche. These innate forces determine what attracts and repels you, as well as what excites and repulses you. As such, your heroes and villains become mirrors of your inner self. What you strongly deny defines you as much as what you passionately affirm.

How does your body figure in your script?   When you were a child, did either of your parents teach you that parts of your body are shameful? Did anyone ever make fun of your body? Did peers or family members ever make inappropriate sexual comments about your body? Did your parents avoid hugging you? Or did your parents teach you to appreciate your body? Have you ever gotten what you wanted by using your looks? What is your body image? Do you like or dislike your body? How does your body image shape your daily behavior? What themes in your script concern your body?

What behavioral patterns do you repeat over and over?   Are you shy and withdrawn? In social settings, for instance, do you cower in a corner? Are you the life of the party? Do you keep getting into trouble? Do you typically procrastinate in fulfilling your responsibilities, or do you always jump in and complete assigned tasks early or on time? Do you often break your promises, or are you dependable? Do you frequently insist on your own way with others, or do you let others decide for themselves what to do? How do you generally behave in a crisis? How do you typically handle disappointments, successes, surprises, or boredom? What words would your closest friends use to characterize you as a person? What do you normally do that reinforces this characterization?

After you've isolated your recurring behavior patterns, trace them back to your original family. Were these patterns developed as a way to cope with particular circumstances? How did the patterns help you survive and thrive in your family? Do they help or hinder you in present life? What would happen if you stopped repeating the patterns?

Now that you've identified your behavior patterns, you can use them to uncover the basic plots and subplots of your script. These plots contain specific situations that call for your recurring behaviors. What are the major plots in your drama? When and how often do they emerge?

How is spirituality woven into your life script? Do you avoid or nurture your spiritual dimension? Who or what are your authorities? Do you feel at home in the universe? Do you feel like an alien in the world? If you pray, do you tend to repeat the same things in your prayers? Are you actively involved in a church or religious group? Does your faith actually influence how you behave from day to day? Do you mold your religion to your lifestyle? If you always want things to go your way, do you understand faith as getting you what you want? Does your spirituality enhance your appreciation for the ideas and values of others, even if they differ from your own? Does your spirituality diminish your understanding of, and appreciation for, others who are different from yourself? Are you dogmatic and rigid? Are you afraid of alternative beliefs, ideas, and religious practices? What creates this fear? Are you intrigued by alternate beliefs, ideas, and religious practices? What stimulates your interest?

How did your original family influence your spirituality? Is your original family and extended family religious? How are your current beliefs and practices different from those of your family?

What aspects of spirituality do you value? What aspects do you think are unimportant? What aspects do you doubt? Is your spirituality compatible with your basic life position?

How does your script define your gender? If you are male, does your script call for you to be strong, brave, unemotional, logical, and tough? Is it more masculine to prefer athletics to poetry and classical music? How much does your masculinity depend upon sexuality? Do you feel positive as a male when you cry? Do you permit yourself to admit weakness and fear? List the qualities that characterize a real male. How many of these came from your family and culture? What did your parents tell you about what boys should and should not do?

If you are female, does your script call for you to be passive, emotional, weak, and tender? What did your parents tell you about what girls always do? Do you feel you're a proper female when you become angry or act assertively? In your opinion, what are the qualities of femininity? How many of these qualities originated in your family and culture?

Considering what your script demands for your particular gender, which of these qualities make you feel uncomfortable? Which of these qualities do you like and value?

Make a list of the major themes, issues, events, emotions, and circumstances that keep recurring in your life. How are all of these related? What do they reveal about your script? Also, what never happens to you that you desire to happen? What do you never attain that you want to attain? What do you never feel and possess that you want to feel and possess? What do the *nevers* disclose about your script?

Rewriting Your Script

Your script is important because it influences what happens in your life. It guides the way you interact with people and respond to events. Your script calls for you to succeed or fail, win or lose, achieve or stagnate, and to feel comfortable or uncomfortable in life. Your script creates the texture and boundaries of your existence, dictating what you should or should not attempt, what you can or cannot achieve, as well as what is and is not taboo for you. This is not the way things really are or the way they have to be; scripts define how you behave in any given situation only when you blindly follow them or believe them to be immutable. The basic nature of any script is that it can be rewritten.

Take Kim, for instance. Kim is single and lives alone in an apartment near her place of work. Because of the circumstances in her original family, Kim decided that something was wrong with her. She felt rejected by her parents and concluded that she was unlovable. This perceived rejection, along with Kim's reactions to it, engendered her script. In subsequent years, she reinforced its basic theme, feeling sure that she would experience numerous rejections. The final act in her script called for her to die alone and despondent.

When Kim entered adulthood, she became highly successful in her career, but continued to follow the childhood script in her personal life. She set herself up to be rejected time after time. She reasoned that if people really got to know her, they wouldn't like her, and acted in ways to keep them at a distance. If others didn't get close to her, she wouldn't be rejected—at least that's the way Kim reasoned.

Picking up on her desire to remain distant, other people eventually ignored Kim; so she was rejected, but not for the reasons she supposed. These sequential rejections over the years confirmed Kim's belief that something indeed was wrong with her as a person. Each time she experienced rejection, Kim's script was reinforced. She believed that she really was unlovable and destined to lead a lonely and miserable existence.

Kim's beliefs about herself and her lot in life have nothing to do with reality, but are all part of the script she fashioned in childhood. That script determines Kim's life course only because she unconsciously follows it, believing it to be the way things really are. If Kim ever questions the logic of the script, and comes to understand that she is reacting to childhood circumstances that no longer exist, she can change the way she behaves and experience a more rich life.

What is possible for Kim is also possible for you. Your script is no more immutable than hers. All scripts can be rewritten to support a more realistic and meaningful life.

Exercise:
Creating an Autobiography

Perhaps you now have a clearer awareness of the script you are living. Once you've identified that script by answering the questions in this chapter, you are ready to embark on a search for your real self at a deeper level, using your script as a launching pad. This exercise will help you discover more about the person who acts out the text, lines, plots, and subplots of your own personal drama.

Relying upon your knowledge of your life script as a guide, create an autobiographical sketch. Pretend that you're a scholar writing an encyclopedia entry about yourself—this will create some distance and make the task easier. You can include whatever pertinent information you choose, but try to differentiate yourself from the script you play. Use what you've learned about your lifestyle and guiding goals to help you identify the recurrent themes that have characterized your life since childhood. Be sure to include your major accomplishments, failures, and unfulfilled dreams, noting how these are basic to your script. Give examples from your past experience to illustrate what parts of yourself are freely expressed in the script, as well as what parts of yourself are denied, distorted, or ignored by the script. When you have finished your autobiography, it is very important to ask someone with whom you feel comfortable to listen as you relate your own story. Telling your story to someone else triggers spontaneous insights and memories that can clarify and enhance your understanding of yourself.

How much of your script was written for you by others and how much of it did you write for yourself? People who write a script for themselves generally experience a higher quality of life than those who either live the script written for them by others or follow a script written to satisfy the desires of others. Does your script allow you the freedom to be yourself—who you really are on the inside—or does it call for you to be who others want you to be?

A musician doesn't become a virtuoso overnight. The development of artistic ability involves playing the same scales, compositions, and exercises over and over again. Technique and expertise emerge from work, dedication, discipline, and rehearsal. As it is with the cultivation of any artistic ability, discovering your authentic self is a never-ending task that demands hours of thinking and rethinking, arranging and rearranging, telling and retelling what you know of your personal story. Each time you relate your story to another, or mentally recalibrate long-held perceptions, you weave together the previously discounted and dissociated parts of yourself into a whole tapestry, a tapestry that becomes more intelligible, challenging, and beautiful with each effort to reclaim it from the depths of your unconsciousness.

Summary

1. People's lives are blended from genetic heritage, environmental conditions, tangible and intangible givens, and individual decisions. Your personal script is one of the most important of the factors that influence who you become.

2. Early in childhood, everyone adopts a style of life and guiding goals. Your lifestyle includes habits, tendencies, and basic attitudes. Your lifestyle controls the substance of your life, and your guiding goal determines its direction. The concepts of lifestyle and guiding goals are essential elements of your life script.

3. Everyone creates a life script in childhood. This script is like the text of a play. It has a beginning, a middle, and an end, including basic themes, plots, and subplots woven throughout the entire text. This script largely determines the course of everyone's individual life.

4. Your script was composed to enable you to survive and thrive in your original family. You did not stop following it, however, when your childhood ended and you left home. People tend to perform their script throughout adulthood, confusing it with who they really are and how they have to live, even though it may no longer produce the results they desire.

5. Your personal script is based on one of four life positions: *I'm okay, you're not okay; I'm not okay, you're okay; I'm not okay, you're not okay;* and *I'm okay, you're okay.*

6. People's scripts are usually unconscious, ensuring that they'll be repeated over and over again. When you uncover your script, two things happen. You understand yourself more clearly, and you can choose to behave differently.

7. Scripts are not immutable. They determine the course and pattern of your life only when you let them. The protagonist of your script is not necessarily who you are or how you have to be. Every script can be rewritten to bring about positive changes in your life.

References

Ansbacher, H. L., and R. R. Ansbacher, eds. (1956) *The Individual Psychology of Alfred Adler*. New York: Basic Books.

Berne, E. (1966) *Transactional Analysis in Psychotherapy.* New York: Grove Press.

Harris, T. (1967) *I'm OK, You're OK.* New York: Grove Press.

Keen, S. (1991) *Fire in the Belly*. New York: Bantam Books.

Stewart, I., and V. Joines (1987) *TA Today*. Chapel Hill, North Carolina: Lifespace Publishing.

4

Family Rules

Human beings are rule makers and rule followers. From the smallest village to the largest cities, people create rules to govern everything from checkers to warfare. Rules are crafted to regulate games, public decorum, grammar, computer programming, the placement of eating utensils on a table, and even how the National Anthem is to be sung. Rules prescribe who can vote and when, who can drive a car, who can get married, who can run a business, and who can practice medicine. Institutions such as hospitals, schools, churches, businesses, and governmental agencies have their own rules and regulations that people must follow. There are even rules that regulate how rules are made and enforced.

Human beings are rule makers because rules make it possible to live in communities without getting in each other's way or violating each other's rights. Rules facilitate appropriate relationships between people and enable society to function properly.

Families—like other institutions—are rule-governed systems. Because rules are inherent in every family system, and because these rules regulate how the system functions, the appropriateness and logic of the rules significantly affects family and individual health. A family that runs by inappropriate, or toxic, rules is less healthy than a family governed by suitable and sound rules. Individuals who grow up in a family regulated by appropriate rules tend to be physically, spiritually, and emotionally healthier than those who live in families with unhealthy and rigid rules. For this reason, understanding the rules in your family system is another way of understanding why you are the way you are and why your original family functioned as it did.

Defining Rules

A family rule refers to any behavior pattern that is indigenous to a family system or relationship. As such, rules describe how individuals characteristically behave or how the family typically functions.

Rules may be created to produce repetitive behaviors or they may characterize unconscious behaviors that are repeated in particular situations. If, for instance, Mom and Dad want their kids to keep their rooms neat, they may enforce the rule that beds must be made every morning. This rule is consciously intended to produce a repetitive behavior pattern. If Sally gets upset and leaves the room every time her husband raises his voice, she is following an unconscious rule that requires her to vanish whenever she thinks her spouse is angry. In this instance, the rule is not intended to produce a particular behavior, but merely to describe it. In both cases, the rules define actions that are repeated over and over again in particular situations.

Family rules can be categorized according to four different poles:

- Overt-covert

- Appropriate-inappropriate

- Flexible-rigid

- Healthy-toxic

How a rule fits these categories determines its affect on healthy functioning in a family system or relationship.

Overt and Covert Rules

An overt rule is one that is openly communicated to family members. Such a rule is given high visibility in the family system, and is usually reinforced by rewards and punishments.

In the Taylor family, for instance, there is a rule forbidding the children to eat in the den. The Davis family, on the other hand, permits eating in the den, but requires family members to take their own dirty dishes to the kitchen. In both families, the rule is clearly stated and enforced by either parent. And although the Davis rule differs from the Taylor rule, both are overt in nature. They were purposely created to sustain a particular state of affairs that is valued by the parents; both rules are clearly and openly transmitted to the children in these households.

Overt rules can apply to any goal or objective held by parents. Usually, these rules regulate who does what household tasks, how the family's schedule is regulated, how family members are expected to interact with each other and people outside the family, how members are to behave in particular situations, and what is or is not permissible.

Unlike overt rules, covert rules are neither clear nor openly communicated to family members. Nevertheless, these rules shape how family members behave in any given situation, and are just as potent as overt rules in determining how the family functions.

In my home, for instance, there is a certain chair that I use in the den. Over the years, my kids have developed the belief that this particular chair is "Dad's chair." They freely use the chair when I'm absent, but they immediately vacate the chair when I walk into the room. I have never told them that no one can use the chair when I'm present. In fact, I always invite the occupant of the chair to keep his or her seat. Yet my words usually have no effect. Whoever happens to be in the chair moves to another one. My children are now grown, but whenever they come back for a visit they replicate the same behavior they practiced when they were much younger. Why do they continue this maneuver? Their behavior is motivated by a covert, or unwritten, rule that only Dad is permitted to sit in this particular chair.

Consider your own family. When you were a teenager and wanted permission to do this or that, did you ask your mother or father (if both parents were around)? Your choice was prompted by a covert rule. If you always asked your mother, the unwritten rule was this: *If you want to do this or that, and you want a "yes" answer, ask Mother first.* If you asked your father first, the rule was, *If you want permission to do this or that, ask Dad first.* The chances are that your parents never instructed you in this matter. Your father probably never sat you down and said, "When you want approval to do anything, ask your mother first. She says 'yes' quicker than I do." Your mother probably didn't say anything like that either. Yet you and any other siblings in your family quickly learned to follow this rule. You observed your parents' tendencies and learned how to make the system work for your benefit. And, having discovered this, you instinctively followed the pattern time and again. This is how covert rules are developed.

The Bostics are a typical middle-class family, composed of mother, father, and two children. Both Mom and Dad Bostic work outside the home, and struggle with the same kinds of problems most families experience inside the home. There is one behavior pattern that the Bostics perform in ritual fashion every evening. At bedtime, Dad is usually reading the paper or watching TV. Mom Bostic is responsible for supervising the kids' baths and seeing that they go to bed on time. She begins by gently reminding the kids to bathe and get in bed. The kids ignore her message. Mom responds with several more reminders. The kids continue to disregard what she says. Their lack of response intensifies Mom's frustration. She gets louder and louder. When this happens, the kids begin to argue until all three are embroiled in a loud squabble. Up to this point, Dad Bostic has been sitting passively in his chair, but his annoyance has been simmering beneath the surface. When he's heard enough, Dad jumps up from his chair with threats about what will happen unless the kids cut it out and do what their mother tells them to do. Reacting to his stern tone, both kids immediately stop arguing and get ready for bed.

There are several covert rules that regulate this bedtime ritual in the Bostic family. Dad lives by this rule: *Try not to get involved in parenting, but when Mom proves ineffectual, come to the rescue with threats.* Mom lives by the rule: *Keep on asking the kids to do what you what them to do, even though they ignore you. If they make enough noise, their father will get them in line by yelling at them.* The kids observe the rule: *It's unnecessary to get ready for bed until Dad yells.*

You'll notice that no one consciously made these rules for the Bostic family to follow. They simply chose—albeit unconsciously—to regulate bedtime in this rather indirect manner. And even though the ritual is uncomfortable for everyone involved, the family continues to repeat the pattern every evening.

This is just one example, but all families are governed by similarly mysterious covert rules. When looked at closely enough, all of these rituals and patterns can be seen to have their own logic. In the case of the Bostics, the mother's ineffectual behavior allowed her to think of herself as sweet and nice, while her husband always stepped in to play the role of "bad cop."

Appropriate and Inappropriate Rules

Family rules, both overt and covert, also can be classified as either appropriate or inappropriate. An appropriate rule is one that accomplishes goals for the common good of the family, and generates healthy behavior patterns. Appropriate goals fit the ages of the family members for whom they are intended, and foster developmental goals. Inappropriate rules do just the opposite. They reinforce dysfunctional behavior patterns, fail to serve the common good, and ignore the ages of the family members involved. Inappropriate rules actually impede developmental progress.

Every family has different values and goals; it is both improper and futile for anyone outside a particular family system to prescribe its day-to-day rules. But, in a general sense, the appropriateness of family rules can be gauged in terms of their efficacy in promoting a healthy emotional environment.

The appropriateness of family rules can be evaluated by applying the three questions elaborated below.

What do the rules produce? Do the rules facilitate communication and strengthen relationships among family members? Do the rules foster human growth and development? Do they enable family business to get done? Do they engender cooperation, support, and understanding among family members? Do the rules empower the family to reach its goals? Do the rules embody family values? Do the rules facilitate socially approved and amenable behavior? Or do the rules produce rebellion, resistance, chaos, fear, and low self-esteem? Do they impede personal growth and development, befuddle communication, and fragment family relationships? Do they result in competition, alienation, distance, and hostility? Do they inhibit family members from getting their needs met? Rules that move families toward healthy relationships and personal growth are considered appropriate. Rules that block movement in this direction are inappropriate.

Do the rules fit the family system or situation? Are the rules age-appropriate? For instance, does the family curfew fit the age for individual children? Does a fifteen-year-old have the same bedtime as a seven-year-old? Are the rules made in consideration of each person's age and abilities? Is a four-year-old required to do laundry, or is that task given to an older child? Do the rules enable unhealthy situations? If, for example, Dad is an alcoholic, do the rules call for other family members to collude in denying his problem? Do the rules permit all family members access to their own thoughts, feelings, wishes, desires, and opinions? Or do the rules require everyone to think, feel, desire, and behave identically? Do the rules fit with commonly accepted values? Do they protect individual boundaries? Or do the rules authorize one family member to abuse or mistreat another? Do they fit the stated or undeclared goals of the family? If, for instance, one goal is to develop independence on the part of family members, do the rules enhance that goal or do they promote dependence? Rules that move family members toward tasks and responsibilities that fit their age and development are appropriate. Rules that hinder movement in this direction are inappropriate.

Do the rules foster developmental goals? Erik Erikson has been very influential in defining the developmental goals of the human life cycle (Erikson, 1963). He described eight stages of personal growth, with each stage containing a major task that individuals must master if they are to proceed to the next stage. Erikson's eight stages continue to be useful in charting healthy personality development and effective personal adjustment. They are outlined below.

Developmental Goals

Stage 1: Basic Trust versus Basic Mistrust
This stage extends from birth to one year of age and entails learning to trust as its basic task. The infant learns to trust or mistrust

the environment depending upon how attentive and dependable his or her parents are. Infants who learn how to trust others, as well as themselves, cope better with their environment than those who lack confidence in themselves and are suspicious of others.

Stage 2: Autonomy versus Shame and Doubt

This stage extends from years one to three. During this time, the child becomes less dependent upon the parents and increasingly learns how to control his or her own functioning. Children who fail to master autonomy develop shame and self-doubt.

Stage 3: Initiative versus Guilt

Stage three bridges the age span of three to six. In this stage, the child develops a conscience and takes initiative in pursuing the satisfaction of his needs and wants within the parameters of his or her internalized standards and values.

Stage 4: Industry versus Inferiority

This stage extends from 7 to 12 years of age. School-age children are expected to learn a number of academic, social, and personal skills that are necessary for a successful life. Children who master these skills develop a sense of industry. Those who don't master these skills generally feel inferior by comparison.

Stage 5: Identity versus Role Confusion

Stage five covers the period from 13 to 17. The primary developmental task for kids in this age range is to establish a sense of identity. They must approach the question "Who am I" from several angles. To achieve a sense of identity, a child must already have mastered trust, autonomy, initiative, and industry. When teenagers sift through the various values and roles available to them, they either establish identity, self-acceptance, and self-sufficiency, or they develop role confusion.

Stage 6: Intimacy versus Isolation

This stage spans ages 18 to 24. The major task for this period is to establish and maintain intimate relationships. To accomplish this task, young people must have established clear boundaries between themselves and their parents. If their earlier relationships with parents have been problematic, young people may have difficulty cultivating intimate relationships with others, resulting in feelings of isolation.

Stage 7: Generativity versus Stagnation

This stage stretches from 25 to 50 years of age. During this period, adults struggle to be creative and productive in both family and career. Those who succeed in this task are said to be generative. Generativity calls for mastery of all the skills learned in the previous life stages. The alternative is stagnation.

Stage 8: Ego Integrity versus Despair

The final stage includes the period from age 51 to one's death. The task here is for individuals to achieve self-completion, or ego integrity. People master this task when they have reached their family, personal, and career goals.

Erikson's eight stages of developmental goals find an echo in the theories of several other researchers who have advanced the field of human development. Examples include moral development (Kohlberg, 1969), cognitive development (Piaget, 1950), faith development (Fowler, 1981), and self-actualization (Maslow, 1970). The underlying assumption in all these studies is that human beings develop in stages. What happens at one stage of development affects what transpires at all succeeding stages.

Families influence the healthy growth and development of children at every stage through several means. Family rules are a crucial factor. As was mentioned earlier, the efficacy of rules can be measured by examining how they foster developmental goals, or particular developmental tasks. For instance, teenagers must achieve a strong sense of identity, responsibility, and independence. Do the rules in a given family facilitate this accomplishment? Or do the family rules restrict individuality, express mistrust, and foster dependence and insecurity? This test of the efficacy of family rules is valid for all the stages of developmental growth. Rules that foster the goals at each stage are appropriate. Rules that impede or distort developmental growth are inappropriate and often toxic.

Flexibility and Rigidity

Family rules can be categorized according to their flexibility. Rules that are pliable and adaptable can be relaxed or even changed to meet the demands of unusual circumstances. The usual curfew for a teenager, for example, may be relaxed for the prom or a special ball game. A rule prohibiting social activities on school nights may be temporarily set aside for a special concert or community activity. Flexible rules are geared to the needs and development of individual family members. Thus, as a child gets older and grows more responsible, flexible rules are altered to reflect those changes. Families that are healthier and have lower levels of anxiety tend to have more flexible rules than those found in dysfunctional families.

Whereas flexible rules are geared to the needs and development of family members, rigid rules are focused on strict obedience, regardless of the situation or extenuating circumstances. Rigid rules must be followed without deviation. Curfews, for instance, are strictly enforced, no matter what the situation. Such rules are enacted with little regard for developmental growth and are enforced with the same intensity in all situations. In more dysfunctional families, the letter of the law takes precedence over individual needs.

Healthy Rules

Rules that regulate family functioning can be classified as either healthy or toxic. Healthy rules enhance emotional, physical, spiritual, and social well-being. To do this, healthy rules must be both flexible and appropriate. There are, in addition, several other characteristics that determine whether a particular family rule is healthy, and sound (Kitchens, 1991; Bradshaw, 1988). These characteristics are described below.

Healthy family rules are attainable. They can realistically be carried out and are consistent with reality. "You mustn't ever be angry," for instance, is neither attainable nor realistic as a rule. "You must process your anger in an appropriate manner," is a much healthier rule, as this injunction is both attainable and realistic.

Healthy family rules promote openness. Family members should feel free to discuss almost any issue with frankness and candor. They shouldn't be intimidated by fear that either parent will be upset by such discussions. Of course, it is inappropriate for parents to burden their young children with certain topics, such as details of the parent's sex life, or discussions that try to make the child side with one parent over the other. Parents must use discretion and good sense!

Healthy rules confirm a person's inherent worth and dignity. Such rules do not put family members down or make them feel unworthy. To the contrary, healthy rules enhance self-esteem and self-confidence. When limiting rules are imposed on children, it should be made clear that the rule is designed for protection rather than punishment.

Healthy rules foster feelings of unconditional acceptance and love. They require accountability, but in a manner that reinforces the child's basic sense of being loved, even if the parent is sometimes angry. Unhealthy rules create an atmosphere in which the child fears total rejection if rules are broken.

Healthy rules benefit all family members. They are not designed merely for the well-being of the parents or other particular family members. Ideally, family rules are created to nurture the well-being of the children, and the robustness of the entire family system. Healthy rules enable all family members to get their needs met.

Healthy rules permit family members to be different from one another. They don't violate a member's uniqueness or potential for growth and change. Healthy rules should actually facilitate the actualization of every family member's inherent abilities and individuality.

Healthy rules recognize the equal worth of each family member. Even though family members all have different roles, responsibilities, limits of freedom, and amounts of authority, they still must be recognized as having equal worth and dignity as human beings.

Healthy rules are learning tools, enabling family members to discover appropriate, functional, and acceptable behaviors. For instance, rules about brushing one's teeth or taking a bath enable children to learn important lessons about personal hygiene. Rules that require children to ask permission before playing with a sibling's toy, or to keep their stereo from shattering glass or eardrums, teach appropriate lessons about social relationships.

Healthy rules embrace basic freedoms which are the birthright of every human being. These freedoms include a person's right to have his or her own perceptions, feelings, thoughts, desires, and beliefs.

Toxic Rules

Toxic rules are just the opposite of healthy ones. Toxic rules produce "dis-ease" among family members, destabilize family homeostasis, increase family dysfunction, and impede family relationships. Over the past decade, a number of professionals with an expertise in family therapy have explored the negative consequences of toxic rules, especially in co-dependent families (Bradshaw, 1988; Kitchens, 1991; Wegscheider, 1981). Eight particular rules have been isolated that are characteristic of severely dysfunctional families (Subby and Friel, 1984):

1. Don't talk about problems.
2. Don't express feelings.
3. Don't communicate directly.
4. Don't have realistic expectations.
5. Don't be selfish.
6. Do as I say, not as I do.
7. It's not okay to play.
8. Don't rock the boat.

Assessing Family Rules

This exercise will help you assimilate the information about family rules by assessing the rules in your original family.

Divide a sheet of paper into three columns. Label these *Family Rules*, *Overt or Covert?*, and *Intensity 1-10*. You can use this model as a guide.

Family Rules	Overt or Covert?	Intensity 1-10

In the first column, list the major rules in your original family. In the second column, indicate whether each rule was overt or covert. Be sure to include healthy as well as unhealthy rules. Then evaluate the intensity of each rule on a 1 to 10 scale, with 1 being very low intensity and 10 being extremely high intensity. Rules that were consistently enforced have a high intensity, whereas rules that were seldom enforced, or ignored altogether, have a lower intensity. By identifying any unhealthy rules, as well as each rule's intensity, you can gauge your family's emotional health. Families that employ more unhealthy rules at higher intensity levels tend to be more dysfunctional. Families that use fewer unhealthy rules at lower intensity levels tend to be more functional.

Rules and Family Types

The nature of family rules is influenced by the type of family in which they exist. Although every family is unique, there are certain similarities between all families. This observation has prompted some researchers to identify three particular family paradigms, or patterns. These paradigms—autocratic, permissive, and democratic—are mentioned with some frequency in professional and popular literature (Hart, 1987; Popkin, 1983; Dreikurs, 1987; Benokraitis, 1993). Of course, not every family can be defined within one of these categories. Complexities such as social class, ethnic differences, and cultural diversity make discrete, or pure, paradigms almost impossible to find. Nonetheless, the autocratic, permissive, and democratic models are helpful in describing how families generally function and how family rules are used.

The Autocratic Family. The autocratic family is one in which one or both parents rule with absolute authority, in the way in which a dictator rules a country. The parents rigidly dominate the children's lives, using pressure, punishment, and rewards to elicit compliance. Very little responsibility or freedom is vested in the children. They must fit in a mold whose dimensions are predetermined by their parents. Such children lack permission to think, feel, believe, or dream independently of their parents' wishes. This situation makes it difficult for them to establish an independent identity. Rules in autocratic families tend to be inflexible, inappropriate, and rigidly enforced. The intent of the rules is to sustain the children's obedience rather than foster their developmental needs. As a result, children in autocratic families grow up with too much control being superimposed upon them from the outside, and too little freedom to develop an inner locus of control.

The Permissive Family. In permissive families, parents reject as out of hand the harsh and uncompromising stance of autocratic parents. Permissive parents do not accept responsibility for creating the mold to which children must conform. They allow children to chart their own course and do their own thing. Consequently, few boundaries are drawn and these are not managed consistently. Children are given the responsibility for determining their own limits, with little emphasis being attached to order or routine. The stress is on personal freedom instead. The parenting style in permissive families generally results in rules being highly flexible, to the extent of being meaningless. Because children of all ages in such families are given a great deal of responsibility and latitude, any rules that exist may be inappropriate as well. Whereas autocratic families have too much control and too little freedom, permissive families have too much freedom and too little control.

The Democratic Family. As is the case with a democratic society, a democratic family places a high value on equality, freedom, and responsibility. To preserve these values, the democratic family incorporates the right mix of elements from the autocratic and permissive styles. Democratic families allow freedom, but not without limits, and provide limits, but not without personal freedom. In democratic families, the primary focus is on meeting the individual needs of all members and promoting their personal growth and development. Consistent with this emphasis, rules in democratic families tend to be both flexible and appropriate.

Change and Circumstances

There are two essential variables that are critical in evaluating family types. These are the dynamic quality of families in general and the existential circumstances that shape each individual family. At any given moment in a particular family's experience, both of these variables actively affect everything that goes on within it.

Family types are generally not static, but dynamic. They tend to change over time and in differing circumstances. A family that always maintains the same pattern is atypical. Most families shift between being autocratic, permissive, and democratic. At any given moment, a family might assume a structure that includes characteristics of one or more of the types described. This dynamic quality affects family rules in a similar fashion. The rules mirror the typical changes in family structure.

Consider, for example, the Elliot family. The father ruled his wife and two children with unwavering control. Both kids were compliant until the oldest girl reached mid-adolescence. Needing, but not receiving, the freedom to develop her own identity apart from the family, she began rebelling. Following months of conflict and turmoil, the father begrudgingly granted his daughter the freedom she needed, but maintained strict control over his nine-year-old son. In this situation, the Elliot family assumed a democratic stance for the daughter while simultaneously being autocratic toward the son.

Family types are also highly sensitive to what can be called existential circumstances, or the ongoing experience of a given family. Changes either from within or without the family system can affect the style in which it proceeds in a particular situation. An autocratic family might moderate into a more democratic type. Faced with a crisis, a permissive family might fall back on an autocratic style. A democratic family might drift either toward the autocratic or permissive position. Whenever existential circumstances influence the basic family type, there is a concomitant impact on family rules. The rules will become more or less flexible and appropriate.

Rules and Adult Behavior

Because rules regulate how families function on a daily basis, they inevitable influence how family members behave. Over time, the rules become inseparably mingled with one's role and personality. Suzie, for example, is the only daughter among four children. The covert rules in her family require Suzie to be passive in relationships with others, a posture her parents consider more feminine and appropriate for her than the aggressive style of the boys. Although Suzie often feels as tough as her brothers, she masks her strength with a gentle demeanor. Her behavior, in turn, prompts her mother to reinforce Suzie's conduct with such statements as, "Suzie, you're so sweet! You never get angry with anyone." This process, triggered by covert rules, creates an illusion for Suzie that being sweet and undemanding is her basic personality. She sees any urge to assert herself as an aberration. In this manner, the family's covert rules create a substitute for Suzie's real self.

Suzie has continued to buy into this illusion. When it came time to apply to medical school—a field for which Suzie showed real promise—she chose to go to nursing school instead. She explained to her career counselor, "I just wouldn't feel comfortable having to lord it over the nurses and orderlies. I think I'll be better off aiming lower."

Al, a middle-aged corporate executive, grew up as the oldest of three children. Early in childhood, he was designated as the family hero. Among other responsibilities inherent in that role, his parents expected him to set an example for this brother and sister. Describing his original family, Al recalled the lecture his mother delivered before every visit to their Aunt Wilma. Wilma's house was cluttered with knickknacks. To prevent Al from accidentally breaking one of these objects, his mom always reminded him never to touch anything in his aunt's house. After recollecting this childhood rule, Al remarked, "You know, even now when I'm browsing in a store that has breakables on the shelves, I walk around with my hands in my pockets." Although Al left his original family 32 years ago, he continues to follow many of the rules imposed by his mother.

Suzie and Al illustrate the long-term potency of family rules. Even in adulthood, long after their original function has become obsolete, many childhood rules continue to be followed. I became aware of this fact when Art, my second child, was in the first grade. On his first day of school, without even thinking about it, I passed on to Art a decree my father had given to me when I started school, and which I also gave to my oldest daughter, Suzanne, when she began school. "I expect you to mind your teacher. And remember, if you get a spanking at school, you'll get another one when you get home!" To the best of my knowledge, I uttered this decree exactly the way my father delivered it to me.

Several weeks after school began, I was joking with Art and pretending to be angry. I reminded him of the "Blevins decree" and announced that I'd have to spank him because he got a spanking at school that day. Art was astonished. He looked at me with wide-open eyes and asked, "How did you know?" At that point, I was the astonished one and the joke ceased to be fun. I found myself in the position of needing to reevaluate a family rule that was at least two generations old.

I chose not to repeat the punishment that Art had received that day in school, opting to follow the principle that a person should not be penalized twice for the same crime. This decision followed a hasty mental assessment of the Blevins decree. Where did my father get that rule? Was it something his father told him on his first day of school? But, more important, why did I pass that rule along to my two oldest kids without judging its value? I concluded that I had done so merely because the rule had been given to me—and that was not sufficient reason to perpetuate it in my own family. The fact that I did give the decree to my oldest kids illustrates how parents unconsciously replicate rules from their original family. I don't know how far back among my ancestors the Blevins decree goes, but I certainly hope that it passed from existence with Suzanne and Art. I did not pass on the rule to my two youngest kids, Alan and Kym, when they began school.

Individuals commonly identify with family rules to the extent that the rules become behavioral patterns. These patterns are repeated throughout life, and are often confused with one's basic personality. Covert rules are especially at risk for this pattern of repetition. Such rules usually operate at an unconscious level, and are reenacted spontaneously, without thought or intent. You merely behave a certain way in particular situations because you have always behaved this way in similar circumstances. This is why Suzie, even as an adult, behaves passively when she is irritated. She does so automatically, without analyzing her behavior. This is also why Al strolls through shops with his hands in his pockets, even though he is a careful and dexterous adult. Such behavioral patterns can be modified with effort and patience. To do this, one must be aware of the patterns and have a strong desire to change them.

Exercise:
What Are Your Rules?

There are two common axioms about the impact that rules have upon family members. The first is that children live what they learn from the rules that regulate what goes on in their family. The second is that adults tend either to repeat the rules of their original family, or rebel against the rules and do just the opposite of what they would dictate. In either case, the rules of your original family have a profound effect upon how you live your adult life.

Nick, for example, is a 40-year-old man who grew up in an alcoholic family. As is typical of such families, denial and secrecy were the primary values of his family system. To conceal his father's drinking problem, Nick's parents did not maintain many friendships outside the family, and seldom invited guests into the home. They also discouraged Nick from having his friends over. Nick complied with their wishes because he was protective of his father, as well as being embarrassed by his behavior when drinking.

In addition to the overt gestures of secrecy coming from his parents, Nick also detected a covert secrecy rule. Whenever Dad was drinking, all hell broke loose if Nick said or did anything that upset his father. Consequently, Nick learned to suppress his emotions and muffle his speech. Over time he became an extremely secretive person, even with his friends outside the family.

Following the secrecy rule as a child helped Nick to survive his father's rage. Now, as an adult, Nick continues to be secretive, but doesn't recognize how this behavior relates to his original family or why it triggers frequent quarrels with his wife. He increasingly becomes defensive and rageful anytime she asks him a personal question, even a simple one, like how his day went at the office. Nick is living what he learned as a child, unconsciously choosing to repeat his original family's secrecy rule. His compulsion to strictly adhere to that rule is rooted in the unresolved issues from his childhood, issues whose existence he strongly denies and refuses to address. He claims that he was simply born a secretive person and can't do anything about that.

Nick illustrates the subtle influence that family rules have upon one's characteristic behavior. People sometimes credit behavioral patterns to personality traits when they are actually repeating some overt or covert family rule. If you candidly explore your own family experience, you will probably discover that, in some ways, you have done just the same thing.

To test this assumption, use a separate piece of paper to list three behavioral patterns that you consider to be the most characteristic of yourself. Then ask a close friend what he or she considers to be your most prominent behavioral characteristics. Add these to your list. When your list is complete, process each behavioral pattern in the following manner:

Relabel the pattern. Discard the phrases "behavioral pattern" and "characteristic behaviors." Identify each characteristic instead as a rule. Nick, for instance, might say, "I live by a strict rule of secrecy." Relabeling your behavioral patterns in this fashion makes it easier to differentiate them from your real self.

Trace the rule's history. How were the rules you typically follow molded by the overt and covert rules in your original family? Are the rules on your list a repetition of family rules, the opposite of family rules, or a modification of those rules? Use specific childhood memories to illustrate the history of the relabeled rules on your list.

Assess the value of your rules. Do the rules you follow enhance or diminish the quality of your life and relationships? Use specific experiences to make your assessment. Remember that the rules you live by are changeable. You may continue to live what you learned as a child, but you are free to change if you desire to do so. In any event, it is healthier to consciously choose your rules than to be unconsciously controlled by them.

Summary

1. Families are rule-governed systems. Although particular rules may vary from one family to another, all families are regulated by rules. The rules enable the family to accomplish its goals and execute daily responsibilities so that family members get their needs met.

2. Family rules determine the behavior patterns of individuals in the family. Rules implicitly describe how those individuals characteristically behave or how they are expected to behave.

3. Family rules may be either overt or covert. Overt rules are openly and clearly communicated to family members. A covert rule is not openly expressed. It regulates behaviors that are repeated without being consciously demanded.

4. Family rules may be appropriate or inappropriate. Appropriate rules fit the age and development of the affected individual and generate healthy behavior patterns. The appropriateness of a particular rule may be determined by asking: *What result does the rule produce? Does the rule fit family goals, as well as the developmental goals of the individuals involved? Does the rule foster growth, trust, and feelings of security?*

5. Family rules may be flexible or rigid. A flexible rule is pliable and adaptable. It can change with circumstances. Rigid rules are just the opposite. They are strictly enforced, no matter what the situation happens to be.

6. Family rules may be healthy or toxic. Healthy rules foster emotional, physical, spiritual, and social well-being. Toxic rules destabilize family homeostasis, impede relationships, and produce low self-esteem, mistrust, and fear among its individual members.

7. Family rules tend to mirror the type of family in which they are active. There are three main types of families: autocratic, permissive, and democratic.

8. Family rules in your original family tend to be repeated in adulthood. In this manner, rules sometimes masquerade as a limiting definition of your personality.

References

Benokraitis, N. V. (1993) *Marriages and Families.* Englewood Cliffs, NJ: Prentice-Hall.

Bradshaw, J. (1988) *Bradshaw On: The Family.* Deerfield Beach, FL: Health Communications.

Dreikurs, R., and V. Soltz (1987) *Children: The Challenge.* New York: E. P. Dutton.

Erikson, E. H. (1963) *Childhood and Society.* New York: W.W. Norton & Co.

Fowler, J. W. (1981) *Stages of Faith.* New York: Harper & Row.

Hart, L. (1987) *The Winning Family.* New York: Dodd, Mead & Co.

Kitchens, J. A. (1991) *Understanding and Treating Codependence*. Englewood Cliffs, NJ: Prentice-Hall.

Kohlberg, L. (1969) "Stage and sequence: The cognitive-developmental approach to socialization." In *Handbook of Socialization Theory and Research*. Chicago: Rand McNally.

Maslow, A. H. (1970) *Motivation and Personality*. New York: Harper & Row.

Piaget, J. P. (1950) *The Psychology of Intelligence*. London: Routledge & Kegan Paul.

Popkin, M. H. (1983) *Active Parenting Handbook*. Atlanta: Active Parenting, Inc.

Subby, R., and J. Friel (1984) "Co-dependency—A Paradoxical Dependency." *Co-dependency: An Emerging Issue*. Pompano Beach, FL: Health Communications.

Wegscheider, S. (1981) *Another Chance: Hope and Health for the Alcoholic Family*. Palo Alto, CA: Science and Behavior Books.

5

Togetherness and Separateness

Let me guide you on a journey from an obscure philosophical concept to a practical, down-to-earth way of viewing personal relationships in your family. The concept is called *harmonia*, a Greek word from which *harmony* derives, and comes from the writings of Heraclitus, an ancient philosopher.

Heraclitus argued that the universe is constantly changing. He illustrated this point by asserting that you can't step into the same river twice. This is true, because nothing is the same from moment to moment. The water that you might have stepped into a moment ago is now downstream and other water has taken its place.

If everything in the world is constantly changing, why isn't there chaos rather than unity and stability? According to Heraclitus, everything that makes up this changing world can be explained in terms of a dynamic equilibrium between apparently opposing forces.

I use the word *apparently* because Heraclitus believed that opposites are actually two connected, or balanced, aspects of the same thing, rather than two separate, contradictory things. He called this connection between opposites *harmonia*.

Heraclitus demonstrated his theory in several ways. On a circle, for instance, the beginning and end, which might seem to be different, are actually the same point. Day and night are not two separate entities, but two aspects of the same temporal continuum. In a similar fashion, hot and cold are distant settings on the same thermal circuit rather than conflicting sensations. This is also true for wet and dry, fast and slow, and even up and down. A road that runs up simultaneously runs down. Up and down are not distinct opposites, but two extreme positions on the same continuous line.

In one way or another, everything you experience is held in balance by opposing forces. Melody emerges from the interplay of harmonious and dissonant sounds. High-wire performers are able to stay on the wire by achieving *harmonia* between the weight of their own body and the force of gravity. You keep control of your car on a steep curve by balancing centripetal and centrifugal forces. You maintain equilibrium when walking or running by preserving *harmonia* between the forces of action and equal but opposite reactions. In psychoanalytic terms, you protect the integrity of your ego by creating *harmonia* between the demands of the id and superego.

The concept of *harmonia*, the balancing of two opposing forces, explains numerous polarities of human nature and experience, including love and hate, consciousness and unconsciousness, psyche and soma, yin and yang, animus and anima, good and evil, male and female. Whenever opposing forces are counterbalanced, *harmonia* is preserved. Whenever the connection between opposing forces is unbalanced, *harmonia* is dissolved and confusion, or disharmony, results. This principle applies to such diverse realities as the ecological balance of nature, the regular flow of oceanic tides, the ability of children to effectively manage a seesaw, and the functioning of a family system.

The *harmonia* that connects and regulates apparently opposite qualities also governs human relationships as people move toward each other and then away again in perpetual motion. The process of moving close and distancing occurs simultaneously, and from moment to moment, in all your relationships, fueled by the forces of attraction and repulsion. This happens because human beings have a need to love and be loved, to be cherished and appreciated. Everyone needs to be valued and accepted by someone. This need is rooted in human nature (Maslow, 1970; Fromm, 1956; Jourard, 1974; Kelsey, 1982). Given this condition, individuals feel attracted to others, are impelled to draw close to them, communicate, and respond.

The force that attracts individuals to each other is countered by a repulsive force. This causes people to draw away from others, do things by themselves, assert their individual needs and desires, and be alone. To be a well-balanced individual, you must achieve *harmonia* between attraction and repulsion. If there is too much attraction, you can become overly dependent and smothering in a relationship. If there is too little attraction, you might retreat to a cave and live as a hermit, or remain in society and become antisocial.

In family life, the need to be connected expresses itself in the interplay of two powerful forces—togetherness and individuality. These two qualities regulate every relationship in every family. Consequently, their management has a critical impact on the personality development, as well as the quality of life, of each member of a family system. This is true to such an extent that people severely diminish their sense of identity and personal security whenever they emotionally cut off from family members (Carter and McGoldrick, 1988).

Your emotionally significant relationships are regulated by the interaction of togetherness and individuality. This is particularly true in family relationships, for in families every member is emotionally significant to every other member. Such a connection exists when one person is affected on an emotional, feeling, and subjective level by what another person says, feels, thinks, or does (Kerr and Bowen, 1988). Either positively or negatively, family members continuously trigger emotional responses in each other. Every family functions as an emotional system: its members are always connected to one another, whether or not they're on speaking terms.

Togetherness and individuality regulate relationships in much the same way in which the gravitational tug of the moon governs the ebb and flow of oceanic tides. Gravity is an unseen force that pulls the tides in and out. Togetherness and individuality are invisible forces that maintain the coming together and separation of people in continuous rhythm. These forces determine how individuals feel about, and behave toward, each other. Relationships cannot exist without some blending of these dynamics. Understanding the ratio between togetherness and individuality in your family helps decipher your relationship with every other family member, and the functioning of your family as a whole.

Togetherness and Individuality

Individuality is a biological imperative that impels people to follow their own dictates, be independent, and achieve distinction (Kerr and Bowen, 1988). This imperative is reflected in your motivation to feel, think, and act for yourself. It is also mirrored in any indifference you may feel about whether others think, feel, or act the same way you do. The individuality force is a factor of the amount of energy you use to run your own life.

There are various biological and psychological systems that permit each person to function as a separate entity. The biological impetus toward individuality is evident in all of human development, from the moment of childbirth. After nine months of developing in its mother's womb, the child makes an abrupt entry into the world. When the umbilical cord is cut, the newborn begins functioning as a separate being. Of course, the infant continues to be dependent upon its mother to fulfill all its needs; but all the biological systems are in place that will eventually allow the child to thrive as an individual. As the child progresses through subsequent developmental stages, he or she increasingly detaches emotionally from the family, ultimately leaving home as a young adult ready to establish an individual life. This drive toward individuality is inherently rooted in human nature.

Togetherness is also rooted in biology. It is the force that urges individuals to follow the dictates of others, recognize their own dependence and connectedness, and function as part of a community (Kerr and Bowen, 1988). This urge is reflected in your ambition to think, feel, and act like others. It is also mirrored in the desire to have others think, feel, and act like yourself. The togetherness force is a factor of the amount of energy you invest in relationships with others.

As is the case with individuality, there are biological and psychological mechanisms that drive people to function as part of a group. These mechanisms account for individuals establishing and cultivating friendships, becoming members of cultural or religious groups, wearing designer clothes or using name brands, and being susceptible to the herd instinct in general (running when others run, panicking when others panic, and so on). These same biological forces also propel individuals to mate and create a family.

Togetherness-Individuality and Relationships

Optimal human functioning can take place when there is an ideal balance between individuality and togetherness (Kerr and Bowen, 1988). Several observations are useful in describing how these forces regulate relationships:

Not everyone has the same degree of need for either togetherness or individuality. Depending upon how individuals responded to their original family system, one person may have a greater need for togetherness, while another has a stronger need for individuality. People's needs for either togetherness or separateness vary over time, mirroring the circumstances in their life. This fact influences the rhythm of relationships, as one person draws closer and the other pulls away.

A balance between togetherness and individuality must be struck in any stable relationship. An important personal relationship is in balance when each person invests an equal amount of togetherness in the alliance and retains an equal amount of individuality (Kerr and Bowen, 1988). This balance is often found, as people gravitate toward others who are willing to make a similar investment of energy, time, and commitment in a relationship. This investment includes the feelings, thoughts, emotions, fantasies, conversations, dreams, and actions centered around the other person. It is important to recognize that negative thoughts, feelings, fantasies, behaviors, and the like can bind two people together as strongly as positive thoughts, feelings, and actions. Both comprise the overall energy that is invested in relationships.

Partners in a close personal relationship constantly monitor the balance of togetherness and individuality in their relationship. Balance in an emotionally significant relationship is never static. It is always changing from moment to moment. This variability is contingent on the life energy that people are willing to invest in a relationship at any given time. Some individuals invest more than others. If

one person invests too much, the other may feel smothered or threatened by the loss of individuality. Whenever one person invests too
little, the other is likely to experience fear of rejection, neglect, and
abandonment. Consequently, both partners in a relationship constantly
monitor each other for signs of change. Each one is attuned to whether
the other is investing too much energy in the relationship or too little.

**Whenever a relationship is unbalanced by too much or too
little togetherness or individuality, the partners automatically respond with attempts to restore balance.** Signs of too little involvement trigger automatic attempts to restore balance by promoting togetherness. Signs of too much involvement trigger automatic attempts
to ensure individuality by promoting distance. Each person's response
is in reaction to the other's. In this sense, neither action can be understood adequately apart from the context of the relationship.

Mitzi and Ken's experience illustrates this process. Mitzi observed that Ken was withdrawing emotionally from their relationship.
She was threatened by his distancing, and automatically reacted by
inviting him to do more with her, and probing him to talk about what
was going wrong. Unfortunately, Mitzi's desire for more contact with
her husband only exacerbated his urge to distance himself. Ken was
going through an identity crisis which had very little to do with his
marriage. As Mitzi frantically reacted to restore togetherness, Ken only
strived harder to achieve some sense of separateness. Mitzi attributed
Ken's withdrawal to his indifference toward her needs, and obsessed
about her own inadequacies as a wife. When her attempts to draw
them together failed, she cried and accused Ken of not loving her.
Mitzi's emotional outbursts only frightened Ken, who was already
feeling inadequate and insecure. What little sense of individual identity he had was being smothered by her efforts to draw closer, which
only prompted him to distance himself even more. Before they could
restore balance to their relationship, this couple had to acknowledge
the basis of each other's reactions, and to discover an appropriate mix
of the togetherness-individuality forces in their marriage.

Sameness and Difference

The togetherness and individuality forces manifest themselves
in two ways. One way regulates closeness and distance in a relation-

ship, as illustrated by Mitzi and Ken. The other manifestation has to do with the emotional needs that individuals have for sameness and difference.

Earl and Becky met during their junior year at college. They quickly became an item on campus. They explained their love for each other as a natural result of all they had in common. They enjoyed the same recreational activities, shared the same values, and came from similar backgrounds. They liked the same foods, television programs, and music. Earl and Becky were alike in so many ways, they believed their marriage to have been arranged in heaven.

Shortly after their wedding, it began to dawn on them that they were not exactly alike. Becky and Earl had significant differences they hadn't noticed before. They had different ideas about what time to get up on Saturday mornings, what brand of toothpaste to buy, and where to eat when they went out. Over time, the differences began to appear in more critical areas, such as previously unexpressed values and personal goals. Earl discovered that Becky did not want children and had no intention of being a traditional housewife. She preferred to have a career outside the home. Earl began to question whether this was the same woman he thought he had married. He had always planned on a traditional family, and had thought that Becky shared his image of the future. Now he wasn't at all sure whether he had married the right person.

Becky also discovered some traits in Earl that heightened her anxiety about their relationship. Earl was a workaholic. He put most of his energy into his career and no longer seemed to enjoy sharing activities or spending time with her. This triggered feelings of rejection in Becky, as well as questions about their suitability for each other. She also began to wonder whether she had married the right person.

Like Earl and Becky, most people base relationships and friendships on a notion of sameness. They pursue common goals, enjoy the same activities, share comparable values, and possess similar personality traits and backgrounds. As relationships develop, however, differences always emerge. Over time, these differences can generate anxiety and spawn conflicts and disillusionment.

It's easy for partners in a relationship to feel threatened when their sameness diminishes. Some particularly stable and flexible relationships provide the freedom necessary for both partners to be clearly individuated yet closely connected. Other relationships cannot afford the tolerance needed for each person to be different or to develop differences. Each relationship has its own *disparity tolerance* expressed as an openness to change and an acceptance of differences.

People who have a high need for togetherness generally have a high need for sameness. Their disparity tolerance is low. As differences surface between the partners, anxiety rises, and one partner attempts to reduce the anxiety by demanding more sameness and less difference.

People who have a high need for individuality have a concomitantly high need for difference. Their disparity tolerance is also high. As sameness is accentuated in a relationship, their anxiety rises. Such people reduce their anxiety by demanding more individuality, or separateness.

I've noticed that young lovers frequently have a low disparity tolerance in their relationship, expecting or demanding a considerable amount of sameness. These couples usually avoid doing or saying things that might displease each other. They want to spend as much time as possible together, and do not handle separations very well. It's not unusual for one person to be overwhelmed by anxiety if his or her partner chooses to do something alone or go somewhere with other friends. Over time this low disparity tolerance may moderate a bit, permitting more freedom for the partners to follow their own separate interests. But people usually do not change much in their basic ability to tolerate difference and change in a relationship.

Whether its disparity tolerance is low or high, a relationship remains balanced as long as the anxiety generated by differences does not exceed the tolerance level. Once anxiety exceeds that level, the relationship loses its balance. The experience of Earl and Becky illustrated this point. Each could tolerate the anxiety created by differences as long as these were limited to trivial issues like toothpaste and eating out. Differences in personal goals, however, generated an intolerable amount of anxiety. At that level, both partners felt the relationship to be threatened.

A person's tolerance for disparity influences the strength of the relationship that he or she is able to sustain. When two persons with similar tolerance levels enter into a close relationship, their alliance usually will not be threatened by disparities between them; their need for sameness and difference is about equal. When two people with incongruous tolerance levels form a relationship, their union will be out of balance until they negotiate a mutually acceptable disparity level.

The need for sameness in families operates the same way as it does with couples. Families, like individuals, have their own level of tolerance for disparity. Anxiety generated by differences among family members is tolerated so long as it doesn't exceed the family tolerance level. Whenever anxiety surpasses that level, family members will spontaneously react to stimulate more sameness.

Families with low disparity tolerance demand more sameness and permit only limited differences. Such families permit very little freedom for members to feel their own emotions, think their own thoughts, embrace their own values, dream their own dreams, or hold their own beliefs. In autocratic families, for instance, the father might declare that everyone will dance to his tune as long as they eat at his table and sleep under his roof. The unspoken message is that family members must be the same as Dad or face exclusion from the family.

Parents enforce their demand for sameness in numerous ways. "Forget the idea about being an artist. You'll be a teacher like everyone else in the family!" "We don't talk about that in this family." "That's a stupid idea!" "As long as you live here, you'll do as I say." "As long as you're a member of this family, you'll think what I tell you to think." Statements like these are designed to inhibit individuality and enforce sameness.

Whenever the demand for sameness becomes intolerable for individual family members, they will spontaneously react to reduce their anxiety. Such reactions follow one of four common behavioral patterns:

1. Compliance

2. Rebellion

3. Combativeness

4. Emotional cut-off

(Kerr and Bowen, 1988; Richardson, 1987)

Compliance. Some people respond to the demand for sameness by complying. They deny the presence of any conflict in the family, suppressing their own desires, thoughts, and feelings in order to meet family expectations of conformity. Such individuals typically engage in a practice called *deselfing*. They give up their individuality to mold themselves to the wishes of others (Lerner, 1985). Over time, those who deself experience diminished love toward the one who demands sameness, become chronically angry, and are candidates for a wide array of psychosomatic and emotional disorders.

Edna had been married to Ralph for 14 years when she developed an ulcer. During the marriage, she routinely put her own desires, interests, and needs on a back burner to comply with Ralph's decrees and wishes. In every marriage, there are inevitable differences that call for negotiation and compromise. This give-and-take is equally shared in healthy relationships. This was not the case with Edna and Ralph. Whenever they had differences of opinion, Edna usually ended up doing things Ralph's way.

Edna never learned how to be assertive with Ralph or to stand up for her own needs and interests. She continuously repressed some very potent emotions, including anger, hurt, frustration, and loneliness. When Ralph opted to go on a four-day fishing trip alone on their twelfth wedding anniversary, Edna began a two-year battle with depression. During this period, she increasingly distanced herself emotionally from Ralph, a tactic that only compounded her mental distress and feelings of alienation. Ralph responded to her emotional withdrawal with frequent outbursts of rage and by spending more time away from home. After several months of interpersonal turmoil, Edna visited her physician, complaining of stomach pains. The doctor began treating her for an ulcer and suggested that she see a counselor. In this way, Edna discovered that her emotional and physical distress were symptomatic of 14 years of compliance in her marriage to Ralph.

Rebellion.   When the demand for sameness becomes intolerable, some people react by rebelling. The onset of rebellion is usually covert, but it sometimes erupts into open conflict. People who respond to the demand for sameness in this fashion often give the appearance of complying with the orders, rules, or wishes of the family authority. Yet, whenever they are alone, they do just the opposite of what is decreed. This was the experience of Nan, a 17-year-old in an upper middle-class family.

When Nan entered adolescence, she was a well-behaved child who never gave her parents a moment of trouble. As she progressed through her teens, however, she demanded increasing amounts of freedom to control and run her own life. Her mom and dad were threatened by these demands, not recognizing them as a normal part of Nan's psychological development. To handle their own anxiety, the parents became stricter, assuming that more control on their part would diminish Nan's desire for freedom. This move only intensified Nan's anxiety, and she reacted by becoming even more intractable. Both Nan and her parents were stuck in a distressing cycle that was soon whirling out of control. Her rebellion did not result from her being a bad child, but was rather a desperate, unconscious effort to gain some freedom from her parent's excessive control.

Combativeness. Some people respond to the demand for sameness by being combative. When they perceive their individuality in jeopardy, they reduce the resultant anxiety by going on the attack. Unlike those who comply without a whimper or who rebel by promising compliance then doing the opposite, combative people fight back. They are highly reactive to any demand for sameness that exceeds their tolerance level, and do not hesitate to voice their disapproval and resistance.

The Gibson family learned about combativeness when the oldest son, Jack, became a teenager. Like all teenagers, Jack needed the proper combination of freedom and boundaries to help him develop his own identity. But the rules set by his parents didn't afford Jack enough freedom. He felt emotionally thwarted by them, and reacted by engaging his parents in arguments over everything they asked, including the most trivial issues. The Gibson household became a battlefield. There were endless accusations and put-downs, as Jack labeled his parents as dictators, and they criticized him for being a spoiled brat. It was not uncommon for these arguments to end in Jack retreating to his room and slamming the door. No one in the family realized that Jack's combativeness was his unconscious attempt to gain emotional distance from his parents and begin to establish an independent identity. The distance provided by the conflicts enabled Jack to reduce the anxiety he felt over his parents' demand that he be exactly who they wanted him to be.

Emotional cut-off. Emotionally cutting off is an alternative response to excessive demands for sameness. This behavior can be expressed in various ways. Whenever anxiety in a relationship reaches a critical level, the person under pressure to conform might walk out of the room, or leave the house for a few hours, or even spend the night elsewhere. The cut-off, however, isn't always geographical. A person may simply shut down emotionally. In this situation, the person occupies the same room or house with the other, but minimizes communication and other interactions.

The practice of emotionally cutting off from a relationship can last for indefinite periods of time. If the anxiety level is moderate and the threat to individuality is minor, the cut-off might extend from a few minutes to a few hours or days. If the anxiety level is high and the threat to individuality is significant, the cut-off can last a lifetime.

This was the case with Al, a 34-year-old draftsman who now lives in California. Al grew up in a small Southern town. His father was an abusive alcoholic who controlled his large family with his rage and tyrannical rule. Whenever Dad was home, Mom and the five kids were expected to behave exactly as he wished. This meant that the kids had to stay in their rooms and be quiet. They were not even permitted to speak at the dinner table. Whoever dared ignore Dad's rules received a beating. The children were so traumatized by their father's behavior that their relationships with each other were also colored by violence and abuse.

The day after his seventeenth birthday, Al left home and hitch-hiked to California. He supported himself with part-time jobs while going to school. After graduation, he married a young woman he met at school and obtained a position as a draftsman. Although Al has achieved some success in taking control over his own life, he remains emotionally cut off from his original family. He sends his mother a card every Christmas; but, since the day he walked away from his chaotic family life, he has never communicated with his father nor with any of his brothers and sisters.

Individuals usually respond to intolerable demands for sameness with one of the four behavioral patterns described above. It is also common for people to shift from one pattern to another, given the changing dynamics in every family system. A child, for instance, might comply before age 12, but become combative or rebellious in adolescence. Another child may start out combative but switch to emotional cut-off in adolescence. The different children in a family can adopt as many different patterns for reducing the anxiety caused by demands for conformity. One child might be compliant, another rebellious, and yet another combative. It is even possible for one child to progress through all four behavioral patterns in sequential order. The nature and intensity of the patterns can vary with each individual's experience, as well as with their perceptions of what is going on in the family. Changes in the family's emotional climate exert an inexorable influence on what behavioral pattern a family member may choose at any given time. These choices go a long way toward shaping the personality that family members create for themselves.

Measuring *Harmonia* in Relationships

Relationships tend to be healthier when there is *harmonia* between togetherness and individuality, sameness and difference, *I* and *we*. Whenever *harmonia* is out of balance, relationships become unhealthy and problematic. This principle is simple to understand, yet in actual experience it is often difficult to establish and maintain. The following set of exercises is designed to help you evaluate *harmonia* in your present relationships in light of the *harmonia* that existed in your original family.

First consider this example. After marriage, Helen and Al had considerable difficulty establishing *harmonia* between togetherness and individuality. Having grown up in a permissive family in which everyone was permitted to do his or her own thing, Helen entered the marriage with a strong need for togetherness. Al came from the opposite situation. His was an autocratic family in which everyone had to do as he or she was told. Al entered marriage with an excessive need to assert his individuality. As a consequence, the couple was unable to balance their relationship. Helen's need for togetherness reinforced Al's fear of being smothered. Al's demand for individuality triggered Helen's fear of being abandoned.

If Helen's and Al's needs for togetherness and individuality in the first years of marriage were placed on a scale, it would look like this:

Togetherness   1 ② 3   4   5   6   7   8 ⑨ 10   **Individuality**

            Helen   *Al*

Over time, and with the help of a marriage counselor, Helen and Al were able to address their unresolved issues with their original families, and established an acceptable *harmonia* between togetherness and individuality. Helen moderated her 2 on the scale to a 4, and Al reduced his 9 to a 7. This did not provide either one with exactly what they needed, but it did create a situation that was more tolerable for both of them.

As you complete the exercise, keep these observations in mind:

1. Every person has a different need for togetherness and individuality.

2. The need for togetherness and individuality varies over time. It is always dynamic, never static.

3. Your need for togetherness and individuality at any moment in a relationship is determined by various factors besides your experience in your original family. These factors include your stress level; snags in the relationship; moments of serendipity; situational factors, such as losing a job, getting a promotion at work, or becoming a parent; and your emotional or physical health.

4. Moderate changes can be made in your needs for togetherness and individuality. You are not likely to make drastic changes from one end of the spectrum to the other—yet you can achieve a more balanced position in your relationships, as did Helen and Al.

Exercise:
Relationships in Your Family of Origin

Rate the balance of togetherness and individuality between you and each of your parents during your childhood. If there were other adults who were closely involved with you as a child, include a rating for them as well. The balance between togetherness and individuality in a particular relationship may have changed over time or in differing circumstances. If this was true, mark more than one scale for that relationship, indicating the time sequence that each represents. Put a circle around the number that best represents your needs at that time along the togetherness-individuality scale. Label the circled number with your name. Then do the same for each of your parents, using a separate scale for each parent. If your needs were the same as one or both of your parents, circle the relevant number and label it with both names (for example, *Josh/Mom*). Underneath each scale, note whether you responded to your parent with compliance, rebellion, combativeness, or emotional cut-off. You can also note other reactions, such as an attempt on your part to draw closer. Draw a box around the rating you would have preferred for yourself in each relationship. Helen's rating would look like this:

Togetherness   1   2   3   [4]   5   6   (7)   8   (9)   10   **Individuality**

Helen   Dad

My Responses: Compliance—I really wanted to draw closer

Togetherness   1   2   3   4   5   6   [7](8)   9   (10)   **Individuality**

Helen   Mom

My Responses: Combativeness

Exercise:
Your Present Relationships

Circling the appropriate number, rate the need for togetherness and individuality in each of your present significant relationships, and note your pattern of responses. Then draw a square around the rating you would prefer in each relationship. Here's how Helen filled out the form after she and Al had therapy:

Togetherness   1   2   3   (4)   5   6   (7)   8   9   10   **Individuality**

Helen   Al

My Responses: Compliance—We're really working on being there for each other in appropriate doses!

Review both sets of scales for similarities and dissimilarities. Are you repeating the patterns of childhood in your present relationships?

Key. Circles represent reality; squares stand for what you would have preferred.

Togetherness 1 2 3 4 5 6 7 8 9 10 **Individuality**

My Responses:

Togetherness 1 2 3 4 5 6 7 8 9 10 **Individuality**

My Responses:

Togetherness 1 2 3 4 5 6 7 8 9 10 **Individuality**

My Responses:

Togetherness 1 2 3 4 5 6 7 8 9 10 **Individuality**

My Responses:

Togetherness 1 2 3 4 5 6 7 8 9 10 **Individuality**

My Responses:

Togetherness 1 2 3 4 5 6 7 8 9 10 **Individuality**

My Responses:

Togetherness 1 2 3 4 5 6 7 8 9 10 **Individuality**

My Responses:

Togetherness 1 2 3 4 5 6 7 8 9 10 **Individuality**

My Responses:

Togetherness 1 2 3 4 5 6 7 8 9 10 **Individuality**

My Responses:

Summary

1. Every person has a need to love and be loved. This need is met by relationships, and these relationships are regulated by two major forces—togetherness and individuality.

2. The forces of togetherness and individuality significantly affect how people feel about, and behave toward others.

3. Individuality is a biological imperative that impels people to follow their own dictates, be independent, and achieve a distinction. The individuality force is a factor of the amount of energy you use to run your own life.

4. Togetherness is also a biological imperative. It is the force that urges individuals to follow the dictates of others, recognize their own dependence and connectedness, and function as part of a community. The togetherness force is a factor of the amount of energy you invest in relationships with others.

5. Every person has his or her own needs for togetherness and individuality. Some people have a greater need for asserting their individuality, while others have a greater need for togetherness and community.

6. For a relationship to be stable, there must be a balance between the forces of togetherness and individuality in each partner. Stability in this context is related to an index called *disparity tolerance*, which measures openness to change and acceptance of differences.

7. Partners constantly monitor the balance of togetherness and individuality in their relationship to determine whether the other is investing an equal amount of energy and commitment.

8. The balance between togetherness and individuality varies over time in any relationship, and partners can exchange roles in terms of being more or less giving and committed.

9. People automatically react to restore balance in a relationship when togetherness and individuality are out of balance.

10. The forces of togetherness and individuality manifest themselves through two dynamics: closeness-distance and sameness-separateness.

11. Families, as well as individuals, have their own disparity tolerance. Families with a low tolerance for disparity react with anxiety when family members fail to conform. Families with a high tolerance for disparity may create anxiety when the individuality of family members is threatened by too much togetherness.

12. Whenever there is a demand for too much togetherness or too much sameness in a relationship, people usually react in one of four ways to preserve their individuality: compliance, rebellion, combativeness, or emotional cut-off. These behaviors help individuals cope with the anxiety created by excessive demands for sameness

References

Carter, B., and M. McGoldrick, (1988) *The Changing Family Life Cycle.* New York: Gardner Press.

Fromm, E. (1956) *The Art of Loving.* New York: Bantam Books.

Jourard, S. (1974) *Healthy Personality.* New York: MacMillan Publishing Co.

Kelsey, M. (1987) *Caring.* Ramsey, NJ: Paulist Press.

Kerr, M. E. (1988) *Family Evaluation.* New York, W.W. Norton & Co.

Lerner, H. G. (1985) *The Dance of Anger.* New York: Harper & Row.

Maslow, A. H. (1970) *Motivation and Personality.* New York: Harper & Row.

Richardson, R. W. (1987) *Family Ties That Bind.* North Vancouver, B.C.: Self-Counsel Press.

6

Generation to Generation

The ancient Greeks told the story of Phaethon, the son of Clymene, a nymph, and Helios, the son god. During his childhood, Clymene regaled Phaethon with tales about his father, whom he had never met. Phaethon boasted about his parentage to his friends, but they wouldn't believe that he'd been fathered by the sun god. Over time, their scorn caused Phaethon to wonder if his mother was really telling the truth. Was he one of the immortals, or was he simply a common boy whose history would end with his own span of years? At 16, Phaethon set out on a journey to find Helios and claim his heritage.

Phaethon journeyed across Persia and India to the palace of the sun in search of his father. When he arrived, he boldly entered the throne room where Helios held court. The sun god gave off a dazzling light. Phaethon was momentarily blinded by the brilliance, which was painful to his eyes.

When Helios saw the youth, he asked in a terrifying voice why he had come. Phaethon answered that he came to find his father. He said that his mother claimed that Helios was his father; but Phaethon's friends had been so scornful of the idea that he himself had begun to doubt whether he was really Helios's son.

Smiling, Helios removed his crown of burning light so the boy could look at him without distress. "Come here, Phaethon," he said. "You are my son. Your mother told you the truth."

There is more to the tale about Phaethon. But this excerpt from the story suffices to disclose a profound truth about personal identity. To find out who he really was, Phaethon had to recover his family origins. In this sense, Phaethon is an archetype for every person who wishes to know who he or she is.

Personal identity is enmeshed with the unique qualities of one's own family, embedded in layers of tradition and emotional issues which have accumulated in one's family system over generations. You discover who you are by exploring your family origins. As Sam Keen has correctly observed, everyone is plural. There is no *I* without *we* (Keen, 1989). This means that you do not make sense as an individual apart from your family. As your shadow is an extension of you, so you are an extension of your family. Your shadow has identity only in relation to your body. In the same way, your identity exists only in relation to your clan.

In the search for yourself, you must inevitably ask two critical questions: *Who are my people? To whom do I belong?* The answer to these questions will enable you to know yourself more fully than an analysis of yourself as a person totally apart. By exploring your own people, you'll discover who you are and why you behave and think the way you do. This is because your family system shaped the way you view the world and how you think about life—even if you designed your outlook to be as different as possible from that of your parents. Within the context of your family, you identified your friends and enemies. Your family indicated whom you could trust and whom you had to obey. Again, these precepts influence you now even if you've chosen to rebel against them completely: they define your rebellion.

From your family, you received traditions about many things—how to celebrate birthdays, when to open Christmas or Chanukah gifts, how to spend a Fourth of July, how to treat your relatives, how to manage your money, and the like. Sometimes these traditions span several generations. And now, as a senior member of your own family, you decide which of these traditions to maintain, which ones to revise, and which ones to discard.

The family system in which you evolved influenced every part of your mind and spirit. It molded your self-esteem, and imprinted your mind with data about what is right and wrong, what is appropriate and inappropriate, what is acceptable or taboo. Your ideas about work and leisure, as well as your sense of duty and your drive for success, were formed in the bosom of your family.

Very early on, your family taught you the way to be close to your parents, siblings, and other relatives. Your family molded your ability to establish relationships with people outside the home, and instructed you about how far you can trust them. Your attitudes toward authorities, peers, neighbors, and foreigners were all shaped by your family. From them you learned to identify life's villains.

Your family, like all families, had its own rules, mores, customs, traditions, rituals, and habits (Keen, 1989). Your family system was a repository for particular themes, emotional issues, and unresolved conflicts that continue to influence the way you think, feel, reason, and behave.

Perhaps you are getting the idea that every component of your being is touched by family influence. If so, this is precisely the point. Although you have the potential to change and grow, your particular course of development was determined by both your genetic inheritance and the massive influence of your family. People are not random creations evolving from a jumble of casual events. Virtually every aspect of your personhood reflects your family's influence, even if you've rebelled universally against everything your family stood for. You can't blame your family for how you've turned out—but you can understand how you've turned out by understanding the context of your family system. Either positively or negatively, your personality bears the stamp of your family's emotional DNA. How you respond to this heritage ultimately determines who you become.

Family Systems Across Generations

Janice was desperate when she called a counselor for help. She was fresh out of ideas, as well as patience, on how to handle her 16-year-old son, Bobby. Janice was exasperated with his grades, selection of friends, overall attitude, and defiant behavior. She had tried everything she could think of to help Bobby, but nothing worked. His behavior deteriorated to the point where he disregarded every family rule and isolated himself emotionally from both parents and his older sister. Two days after he came home drunk, Janice called a family therapist as a last resort. She had given Bobby a final ultimatum: if he came home drunk again, she intended to put him out on his own.

The therapist collected information about the family system. He discovered that Janice's mother had died three years prior to the onset of Bobby's problem behaviors. Following her mother's death, Janice assumed the role of caretaker for the extended family. She functioned as a mediator between her father and brother, who were often at odds, carrying messages back and forth between the two. She went to her father's once a week to stock his freezer with home-cooked food, made sure that he attended to his health, and even ironed his shirts for him. She also assumed her mother's place in caring for an older brother, who had a drinking problem. Janice in effect replaced her mother in the family system, functioning for extended family members in just the same way her mother did.

As the therapist collected data about the family, he extended his inquiry to include the three generations preceding Janice. What Janice revealed about her family system was extremely instructive. Both her mother and grandmother had been strong and energetic women who functioned as the caretaker for their family. Each of these women died young from a coronary disorder. When the mother of each generation died, her role was filled by the oldest daughter from the next generation, exactly as Janice had assumed her own mother's role.

Janice's family system had repeating patterns having to do with eldest sons as well as caretaking mothers. In each of the three previous generations, the oldest son had become uncontrollable and was expelled from the family—the same penalty with which Janice had threatened Bobby.

The therapist helped Janice see how she and Bobby were repeating a pattern ingrained in her family system—a pattern Janice had failed to recognize but was unconsciously replicating. If Janice remained in the caretaker role, she would very likely endanger her health and even her life, as all the other female caretakers had died prematurely from heart disease. Janice confessed to the therapist at this point that she had been under the care of a cardiologist for six months.

The therapist enabled Janice to interpret her problems with Bobby within the context of her own family system. She could repeat the pattern—which called for the oldest son to be banished from home and the caretaker to die of coronary disease—or she could choose to change her part in the system and thereby obtain different results. Janice chose the second option. Under the therapist's supervision, she effectively abrogated her caretaking role and crafted more appropriate ways of relating to Bobby and extended family members. Her physical health improved and Bobby's misbehaviors, which were symptomatic of the dysfunctional family system, disappeared.

Janice's family system is emblematic of all family systems. People and their habits die, but the unique traits of particular family systems tend to live on through the generations. Each succeeding family is never exactly the same, but close analysis will usually reveal the repetition of major themes and patterns. Emotional energies residing deep within the family's collective psyche propel the system with a force that is virtually irresistible. Family members consciously or unconsciously repeat behavioral patterns embedded in the system, or rebel against the system and try to make their lives completely different. One might suppose that the second response would change the system; but that's not what usually happens. One generation's rebellion against family patterns generally results in a replication of those patterns by the next generation. In either case, the family system proceeds intact from generation to generation.

The Generational Process

You are partially the way you are because of heredity. Your genetic inheritance includes a DNA code that simultaneously links you to your ancestors and assures your uniqueness. Consequently, your personhood is understandable only within the framework of your genetic heritage.

You are also the way you are because of your generational inheritance. Various aspects of your personality and ways of being bear the indelible imprint of your family system, ensuring that you possess certain traits indigenous to that system. These traits distinguish you as belonging to a specific people. For this reason, your identity is more fully revealed when your generational heritage is taken into account (McGoldrick and Gerson, 1985; Kerr and Bowen, 1988; Bradshaw, 1988).

If you want to understand why your eyes are a certain color, biological principles of genetic inheritance enable you to do so. The study of genetics reveals more and more as research continues about how heredity works. In a similar manner, the study of your family system across the generations can help you understand why you have evolved into the person you are, and why you respond to life the way you do. Your family system programmed you in several ways, including:

- Conscious definitions

- Family traditions

- Unconscious behavioral patterns

- Family myths and stories

- Individual responses

These basic categories are described below.

Conscious Definitions

Verbal pronouncements are one way in which parents program family members to adopt desired values, goals, expectations, and ways of doing things, or to conform to particular traditions. Sometimes this programming is done explicitly in the name of the family. "Tollivers never lie." "We Chans are a forgiving people." "You're a Johnson, and Johnsons are brave." "If you're going to be a DelSignore, you have to learn how to fight." "The Edelsteins always keep their word." Family rules are sometimes implicit, rather than explicit, in these pronouncements. "Don't ever forget your roots!" "You come from a long line of good students." "Grandparents have always had an honored place in our family." "Men in this family are good providers." "Our women have always been great cooks." "We don't talk about such things in this family."

Whether explicit or implicit, such messages communicate particular values, expectations, and ways of being that are intended to mold the children. When repeated often enough, these messages are imprinted in the child's mind, influencing both behavior and identity.

In addition to passing on family characteristics and expectations, parents also preprogram their kids to have particular personal qualities. Mom might say to Junior, *"You're just like your Uncle Robert. He never finishes anything he starts."* If Junior hears this often enough, he'll believe it to be true—and he *won't* finish anything he starts. Junior doesn't become just like his Uncle Robert because that's necessarily the way he was meant to be. He's simply conforming to his mother's definition of his limitations.

Definitions can involve simple carelessness on the part of parents as they repeat phrases that can have a devastating effect. *"You never listen." "You're uncoordinated just like I am!" "What a slob you are!" "You're tone-deaf like the rest of the family." "You're so smart—you'll always be the best at whatever you do."* Young children take such statements literally, and unconsciously accept them as definitions of their identity. As children grow into adults, they frequently confuse such definitions with their actual personality. Negative phrases can impose tragically unnecessary limits; but even positive phrases can prove burdensome, as in the case of the precocious child who grows up to believe herself unlovable and unworthy unless she continues to excel in everything she tries to do.

Family Traditions

Mark, a friend of mine, grew up in a patriarchal family as the oldest son of an oldest son of an oldest son. There had been oldest sons in his family going back for at least six generations. The accident of Mark's birth order has subjected him to his family's expectations that he would follow their traditions and fulfill the role demanded by the family's generational script.

One of these traditions is associated with an antique shotgun, which symbolizes responsibility and status in the Biddle family. The gun has always been handed down from the oldest son to the oldest son of the next generation. This is how Mark's grandfather came to possess the gun, and Mark's father after him. Mark will become the gun's custodian when his father dies. The potency of this tradition is underscored by the fact that males in the Biddle clan are shooters, not killers. If they do shoot a gun, they aim at tin cans, never at anything alive. In fact, Mark himself is a pacifist and has no utilitarian interest in guns at all. Given this twist to his family script, why is inheriting the shotgun significant to Mark? The gun itself is inconsequential, but it symbolizes a value that is singularly important: common decency and paternal responsibility for the well-being of one's children and grandchildren. Mark has embraced this legacy in his own life and wishes to pass it on to his sons. In this particular family system, the antique shotgun is an emotionally charged talisman that represents paternal responsibility. Handing down the shotgun from oldest son to oldest son is a tradition that implicitly signifies loyalty to the male heritage of the Biddle family.

Family traditions have tremendous power to govern the behavior of individual family members. Such traditions are seldom written down, yet frequently they are as scrupulously observed as if they'd been prescribed by national or state legislation. Sometimes traditions are consciously acknowledged and enforced, as in the Biddle family. In other cases, traditions flourish on an unconscious level, as illustrated by the experience of Janice and her son Bobby. Whether conscious or unconscious, family traditions always embody the values, mores, and ideals of the family system in which they are embedded, and exert an almost irresistible influence on the behavior and attitudes of family members. As such, these traditions constitute emotional road maps for family members to follow, providing them with the "proper" attitudes and behavior.

An endless variety of behavioral practices are covered by family traditions. These practices range from trivial to important matters. Tradition might dictate opening gifts on Christmas Eve or morning, serving Dad breakfast in bed on Father's Day, or letting family members choose the menu on their birthday. There are toxic and harmful family traditions, such as alcoholism, drug use, physical violence, and other forms of abuse. Family traditions can revolve around specific vocations or hobbies, the development of certain abilities, the giving of cherished names to newborns, or participation in particular organizations or movements.

Traditions always exercise an emotional tug on family members. Whether or not they choose to follow a particular tradition, their reaction, either negative or positive, is an acknowledgment of that tradition's power. Family members may feel uncomfortable and inadequate when a hallowed tradition is ignored. Conversely, they may feel relieved and comfortable whenever a prominent tradition is observed, even if the effects of that tradition are negative. Significant traditions are those that elicit the belief "It *has* to be done this way." Such traditions often stimulate conflicts among newlyweds, who each want to do things the way they were done in their original family. The power of traditions commonly asserts itself later in life, when a person says something like, "I promised myself I'd never treat my children the way I was treated, but here I am doing the same thing now!"

Unconscious Behavioral Patterns

Jimmy, a nine-year-old, was referred for therapy by his school counselor because he manifested a profound fear of people and refused to play with his schoolmates. Lucky for Jimmy, the therapist had a specialty in family systems. Rather than assuming Jimmy's behavior to be the manifestation of a psychological disorder, she chose to look at the large picture and treat the child within the context of his family. Through this process, the therapist revealed Jimmy's problems at school as the result of two unconscious behavioral patterns he learned at home.

Jimmy's xenophobia originated from his mother's side of the family. An interview with the mother uncovered a pattern of devastating business failures and random attacks of violence by strangers. Similar experiences characterized the mother's family over a three-generation period. Consequently, the family developed an extraordinary fear of persons, which was built around a core belief that you can't trust people. This belief was transmitted to each new generation through behaviors rather than words. In Jimmy's case, whenever someone knocked on the front door, his mom would peep through the curtain to see who was there. If she didn't know the person, she seized Jimmy, along with his younger sister, and hid in a kitchen closet. She kept the closet light off and instructed the children not to speak. They stayed in the closet until the unknown visitor gave up and left.

Jimmy's mother never told him to be afraid of strangers. Explicit instruction was unnecessary. She communicated her fear of strangers through her behavior, just as her own parents had done. When confronted with the oddness of her behavior, the mother was surprised to learn that it was feeding her son's xenophobia. Becoming aware of that fact enabled her, after getting some therapy herself, to handle her fears in a different way. She eventually was able to teach her children an appropriate wariness of strangers. When this was accomplished, Jimmy's xenophobia disappeared.

Informed by the school counselor about Jimmy's failure to engage in play with his classmates, the therapist decided to look at this, too, in the context of the family system. Even at home, Jimmy didn't play the way other nine-year-old boys played. He "drove" a toy tractor, built things out of cardboard and clay, and always helped willingly with chores. But he never went bicycle-riding, played ball, hide and seek, or other make-believe games. He never asked for a Nintendo game, or for a pair of rollerblades, or to go fishing, hunting, swimming, or to a movie.

As the therapist learned more about the father's background, it became clear that men in this family were all work and no play. Jimmy's father didn't fish, golf, go camping, or ever play cards. When he got home from his day job, he worked on the family farm or around the house. Jimmy's four uncles were just the same—hard-working nononsense men. The pattern also held true for Jimmy's grandfather, great-uncles, and great-grandfather. For three generations, not one male in this family engaged in any leisure recreation—they didn't even watch sporting events on TV. The operational core belief was, "Men in this family work. They never play."

Jimmy's dad never told him *not* to play; and he might not have refused to take him swimming, fishing, or to the baseball game—but Jimmy had never asked. The father was unconsciously enacting the family's core belief about work and play. Early in life, Jimmy observed this model and patterned his own behavior accordingly, assuming that this was the way things were supposed to be.

When Jimmy's refusal to play was understood in the context of his family system, his behavior ceased to appear abnormal. It was quite normal for that particular family. Jimmy was merely behaving as the men did in his family, and in doing so was being a very loyal son. The therapist convinced Jimmy's father to change his habits for his son's sake and engage Jimmy in some real play activities. After the whole family spent time in treatment, Dad became less uptight and Jimmy gladly joined his classmates during playtime at school.

Jimmy's experience is perhaps a bit extreme; but it's a good illustration of how family traditions are perpetuated through unconscious behavioral patterns. These patterns usually manifest themselves as habitual actions which family members repeat without ever thinking about them. An unconscious systemic behavior pattern announces itself when someone can't give a reason for a typical behavior, but can only respond, "I don't know. I've *always* done this." These patterns influence a wide array of personality traits and behaviors, including facial expressions, ways of laughing, physical gestures, styles of walking or running, styles of interacting with others, how and when one cries, speech patterns, and quirks of dialect.

Family Myths and Stories

I have fond memories of my grandfather, whom I affectionately called *Papa*. He was a man who liked to tell stories. One of my favorites was his firsthand account of the New Market train wreck, a nineteenth-century accident preserved in folklore and folk music. Papa was a teenager living in New Market, Tennessee, at the time, and was ploughing a field when he heard the noise of two trains colliding several miles away. A short time later, a neighbor found him and asked if he would go to the site of the wreck and search for her son, who was supposed to be on one of the trains. For several hours my grandfather helped injured victims, and searched among the scattered dead bodies, traumatized survivors, and twisted pieces of iron, looking for the young man. The neighbor's son, however, was nowhere to be found. As luck would have it, he'd missed the train in Knoxville and was sitting in the train station when the wreck occurred.

Until the day he died, I never tired of hearing Papa relate the story of the New Market wreck. Looking back on it now, I realize that there was more to that story than met the ear. Every time my grandfather related what happened on that fateful day, he was silently instructing me about how people in our family respond to a crisis. We don't sit on the sidelines while others are caught in a struggle. Our family system calls for us to leave what we're doing, set aside any squeamishness or fear, and do what we can to help. I have seen the validation of this family precept many times, observing how my mother reacts in a crisis situation. She is strongest when helping someone who is suffering. This is a way of reacting that she learned from her father.

The precept about reacting bravely in the face of adversity did not begin with my grandfather. It is a trait of the Murrin family which goes back for generations. As a loyal member of that family system, my grandfather replicated the trait in his own life. That's why he responded to the train wreck the way he did, immediately and automatically, without thinking about it. His story about the wreck became an unconscious vehicle for passing the family precept on to succeeding generations. That's how it came to my mother, and that's how it was handed down to me. The story of the New Market train wreck is a family myth that says as much about what it means to be a Murrin descendant as it does about two trains that collided decades ago.

Every family has a cache of oral tradition, stories that are unique to the family and are passed verbally from parent to child across the generations. Why is it that some stories are passed on and others are not? What determines the selection of family history that becomes oral tradition? Why do families remember some events and forget others? Family stories survive because they are encoded with family values, ideals, expectations, and assumptions. Although the stories may not openly espouse these components, they still function as family myths, either negatively or positively guiding and instructing members to live according to their family traditions.

Your family's stories tell you who you are and how you are expected to live. They identify family heroes and villains, as well as family values and expectations. They preserve a modicum of family history which enables you to identify yourself. This process of identification is hopeless without the context of your generational heritage. To know what it means to be an American, you must know something about your national history. In the same way, to know yourself, you must know your personal history. This history is embedded in the stories passed across the generations of your family.

Individual Responses

Although families imprint individual members with values, ideals, and expectations indigenous to the family system, the results for the programming depend on how each individual responds. There are two main responses: to honor family traditions or reject them by doing just the opposite. Rebellion against tradition tends to trigger a boomerang effect which causes the rejected tradition to reappear in the next generation. Either way—by honoring traditions or rejecting them—the family system survives intact.

Emotional themes, issues, and characteristics that are present in one generation inevitably surface in succeeding generations. Gail's case illustrates how this works. Gail grew up with a tyrannical mother who was exceedingly harsh and critical. Because of her experience, Gail promised herself that she would never treat her own children in the way she was treated. In time, Gail married and had a daughter. True to her promise, Gail's parenting style was the opposite of her mother's. She was excessively passive and permissive. But far from banishing the family tradition of an emotionally charged relationship between mother and daughter, Gail unwittingly replicated the basically dysfunctional situation; it simply resurfaced in another guise. The generational cycle was completed when Gail's daughter became a mother herself. Feeling that she had never received the structure and guidance she'd needed from her mother, Gail's daughter chose an authoritarian parenting style. Her own children found her to be highly critical, angry, and tyrannical.

Whenever a person rejects a tradition out of hand, the family pattern tends to survive, because the issues basically remain the same. Gail's relationship with her mother was one-up and one-down, with Gail in the one-down position. Her relationship with her daughter became a mirror image of her relationship with her mother, with the roles reversed. By the time Gail's granddaughter came along, the original configuration asserted itself again.

Individuals do have the power to change traits that are embedded in their family system. Yet, when they go from one extreme to the other—from total acceptance to complete rejection—the basic system remains intact and survives from one generation to the next.

Creating a Family Puzzle

You can apply the material in this chapter to your own family in numerous ways. One way that is particularly effective is to create a family puzzle. You do this in much the same way that you work any puzzle, only in this instance you use words and stories rather than separate, squiggly-cut pieces of cardboard. When the various pieces of information are joined together, you will have one view of your family system which will focus on your place in that family as well as the way in which you are carrying on the family traditions. The reason I say that you will have one view of the family is related to another difference between a word puzzle and a physical puzzle. In puzzles that come in boxes, the various pieces join together in only one way. In creating a word puzzle describing your family, the various pieces of information can be joined in several different ways to form new configurations. This means that if you continue to work on your family data, new perspectives and insights will emerge. Understanding your family system as it has moved, and continues to move, across the generations is never a completed process.

The simplest way to create your family puzzle is to use this three-stage process.

Stage 1: Collecting Family Data

The usual way of working a puzzle is to begin by collecting all the pieces, turning them face-up, and perhaps organizing them according to color and shape. Essentially the same process is used in creating a family puzzle. You begin by collecting and organizing separate pieces of information about your family. You can expand this exercise with as much information as you please, but the following guidelines will get you started.

1. On a sheet of paper, list ten traditions of your original family. The traditions may include normal routines, such as opening gifts on Christmas Eve rather than Christmas morning, or taking a vacation in the same place every year. You can describe more exceptional traditions, like the Biddle family shotgun mentioned in this chapter. After you've listed ten of your family traditions, put a check by the ones you consider most unique to, and significant for, the family system. You might find it helpful to ask an older relative why or how this or that was done in your family. Here's an example of what this first step might look like.

✓   1. Make our own cards for birthdays and other holidays.

2. Have Thanksgiving dinner at Mom's house.

3. Always say "I love you" at the end of a phone conversation with a family member.

✓ 4. Read or tell a story to the children at bedtime.

✓ 5. Sing songs to the children.

6. The senior family member has control of the family purse-strings.

7. Everyone in the immediate family should be on friendly terms and stay in touch, even if there are serious disagreements between family members.

8. Adult children should call their parents and grandparents regularly (it's the child's responsibility to stay in touch).

9. Senior family members should be generous toward younger members of the family, helping out financially when help is needed.

✓ 10. We are a family that cares about music and art.

2. On another sheet of paper, briefly describe the main stories passed down to you by older family members about your relatives. If you consider these stories to be examples of what it means to be a member of your particular family, rather than merely tidbits of information, what are the values and unspoken messages of the stories? What do the stories reveal about the character of your family system? This is how one person completed this step:

1. Nana was in love with a pharmacist named Mischa, who emigrated to Argentina, then neglected to propose marriage when he wrote asking her to join him. She came to America instead and married Papa.

2. When Nana came to this country, Papa fell in love with her because she was so beautiful. She never loved him the way he loved her.

3. Daddy went on a canoeing trip with his mother before he got married. The way she told the story, it was the high point of her life. She wasn't yet divorced from Grandpa.

4. On parent-teacher night, Papa went to Mom's school, and the principal told him that she was the dumbest child in

her class. Papa repeated the story to Mom when he got home. He was very ashamed.

5. Before she married Daddy, Mom was in love with a boy named Jasper. He left her for a girl from Oklahoma when he was sent there during the war. Mom married Daddy because Papa told her that he was probably the best she'd be able to do.

6. When Mom brought Freddy home from the hospital, she was afraid to unwrap him. She didn't know for three days whether or not he had feet. Daddy bathed and changed the new baby.

7. Papa's family was so poor that his mother cooked his pet chicken.

8. Grandpa feigned a back injury when Daddy was 13. From then on, Daddy had to support the family.

3. As you think about your family for generations past, or talk with older family members, list the behavioral patterns that keep recurring in your family. You can also use the family stories you wrote down to search for patterns. Perhaps there has been someone in each generation who has been an alcoholic or crippled by some other disorder. Maybe divorce has been a pattern, or possibly the absence of divorce is characteristic of the system. Have the same vocations been adopted by members of successive generations? Family patters can include any behavior: whether family members are close or distant; gender characteristics involving women doing this and males doing that; symptomatic patterns like abuse, suicide, and emotional illness; and matters pertaining to who is a success or failure. You can identify recurring patterns by isolating any particular situation or condition in the family and then determining if it has happened before in previous generations. As you do this, keep in mind that behavioral patterns often skip a generation. See if this is true for any pattern in your family system.

Read through the example, then write your own analysis.

Well, disappointment in love is certainly a pattern.
It also seems as though Mom was sort of set up from
the beginning to feel like a failure. (Is that why I'm

driven so strongly to succeed?) On Dad's side, there's almost a tradition of men being bad at earning a living—Freddy has carried this on without skipping a beat! For three generations, women have stayed for a long time with a man they didn't really love (including me in my first marriage).

4. Write down the major themes of your family heritage. These themes may have taken the form of slogans that were openly taught by your parents or grandparents; or they may have been unspoken, communicated only by how family members reacted in certain situations. Look for the maxims or values that your family considered important, such as "Work comes before play," "Honesty is the best policy," "Keep your feelings to yourself," or "Be strong and never admit your problems." If you can, use specific examples to illustrate each maxim that was handed down to you.

Stage 2: Putting the Puzzle Together

Create a picture of your family system based on the information and ideas you collected in the first part of the exercise. What are your family's basic values, strengths, weaknesses, and characteristic traits? Be as specific as possible in your observations. Write a summary, or work in some other medium to create a picture: use paint, clay, music—whatever feels most comfortable to you. Write a poem, write a detailed analysis, or write a letter to your great-grandparents letting them know how everything has turned out. The important thing is to characterize your family system according to what you've learned.

Stage 3: Identifying Yourself in the Family

You can focus the information about your family by identifying your place in the family puzzle. Using the summary you developed in Stage 2, target the values, traditions, and family characteristics that you are repeating, modifying, or rejecting altogether. What part of the family system do you want to retain? What parts do you want to dispose of? If you have children, what parts are you passing on to them? Remember that rejecting a family pattern by doing the exact opposite often ensures that the pattern will surface in the next generation.

Summary

1. Your identity is ultimately related to your family heritage. This is true biologically—genetic traits are passed from generation to generation—and it is also true psychologically. Psychological traits in a family system are passed on from one generation to the next.

2. People die, but family systems don't. Systems continue across generations to influence many aspects of personality and behavior.

3. Family systems are perpetuated through five main processes: conscious definitions, family traditions, unconscious behavioral patterns, family stories, and individual responses.

4. Conscious definitions are used by parents to mold their children. Definitions may be specifically linked to the family name or to a specific quality. In either case, children generally accept the definition as an unalterable fact. Whether or not the definition describes the child in positive terms, it can be both limiting and burdensome as the child becomes an adult.

5. Family traditions involve numerous behavioral practices that govern the way children behave. Over time, children tend to accept these traditions as the way things are supposed to be.

6. Family members automatically repeat unconscious behavioral patterns. These patterns influence a wide variety of personal characteristics and traits. As one grows older, the patterns are frequently confused with one's real identity.

7. Family stories are present in all families and serve the function of perpetuating values, goals, assumptions, and beliefs. These stories inform family members of their generational heritage. They also evolve into myths that instruct children about life and how it should be lived.

8. The unknown factor in the way a family system is passed on has to do with individual responses. People generally repeat a family pattern, or rebel against the system and do just the opposite of what is dictated by the pattern. In either case, the system remains intact and survives. In order to really change or obliterate a tradition, a person must find an alternative to repetition or rebellion.

9. Despite the extent to which your family system influences your development, you are still responsible for how you choose to respond to the system, its values, and traditions.

References

Bradshaw, J. (1988) *Bradshaw On: The Family.* Deerfield Beach, FL: Health Communications.

Keen, S., and A. Valley-Fox (1989) *Your Mythic Journey.* Los Angeles: Jeremy P. Tarcher.

Kerr, M., and M. Bowen (1988) *Family Evaluation.* New York: W.W. Norton & Co.

McGoldrick, M., and R. Gerson (1985) *Genograms in Family Assessment.* New York: W.W. Norton & Co.

7

Family Dances

As long as 50,000 years ago, people made cave drawings to record their ritual dances. Every tribe and clan of ancient peoples had its ceremonial dances. These marked significant events in the communal life of the tribe, such as the birth of a child, a person's passage into adolescence, the rite of marriage, and the death of a tribe member. Dances were used to stimulate courage for battle, as well as to celebrate a victory. They were also used to dispel emotional distress created by fears, crises, problems, superstitions, and natural calamities. In various forms, ritual dances reduced the anxieties of primitive peoples and restored balance to their lives.

Ancient tribes were not unlike modern families. Families must constantly deal with the imbalances caused by stress and its accompanying anxiety. Stress can result from both negative and positive events: the birth of a child, the loss of a job, a serious illness a move to another city, the death of a loved one, an unhoped-for success. Even if the stressful event initially affects only one family member, the stress soon spreads throughout the entire family unit. When the homeostasis of the family is upset, family members automatically react to the imbalance with redundant behavioral patterns called *dances* (Lerner, 1986). Like the primitive dances of ancient times, these modern family dances serve the purpose of reducing stress so that homeostasis can be restored. If a particular dance becomes a set pattern over time, the dance itself can become a problem that stresses the family system.

Types of Dances

The types of dances used to reduce stress vary from family to family. Generally, they involve a minimum of two family members (a dyad) interacting with each other. The interaction might include the spousal dyad, a parent-child dyad, or a sibling dyad. It's not unusual for one or more dances in the same family to involve different dyads. Families imbue dances with their own distinctive style. They govern how family members interact with each other whenever stress unbalances their relationships.

The Circular Dance

Some couples control anxiety in a relationship by performing a circular dance, a process wherein they repeat the same interactions over and over again. In a circular dance, members of a couple respond to a particular issue or situation by taking the same rational stance, saying the same things, behaving in the same way, and arguing the same point. This triggers a circular wrangle that seldom changes, with each person always saying and doing the same thing. In circular dances, nothing is resolved other than processing anxiety and keeping the two people emotionally connected to one another.

Robbie and Calvin had similar experiences in their original families that had a tremendous impact on their own marriage. Robbie grew up in a family controlled by a chronically angry father. She was the second of three girls in the family and was often the target of her father's rage. From her experience with her dad, Robbie developed the belief that close relationships with men are unpredictable and emotionally hazardous, since men can't be trusted. This belief predisposed

Robbie toward failure in her numerous relationships with males during her young adulthood. These experiences only reinforced her views about men. After years of dealing with her father's capriciousness, Robbie came to see herself as excitable, emotional, irrational, and weak.

Calvin grew up the only child of a single parent, as his father died when he was one year old. Calvin's mother battled with hypochondriasis, a disorder that caused her to focus on her own problems and anxieties rather than on her son and his needs. Calvin's mother was both critical and demanding. Consequently, he came to believe that close relationships with women were painful and dangerous. Like Robbie, Calvin had several turbulent relationships with women which only confirmed his beliefs about females in general. In reaction to his mom's frequent hysterical outbursts, he adopted a relationship style that was cool, unemotional, logical, and distant.

In time, Robbie and Calvin met, dated, and subsequently married. Their marriage, however, was destined to be filled with long interludes of distance, as each one was afraid to draw close to the other. This activated a circular dance that they used to manage the anxiety created by closeness. The dance always followed the same pattern:

1. Over a period of time, Robbie would become increasingly anxious over Calvin's aloofness. As her anxiety increased, she focused upon some trivial issue in their relationship until the thought of that issue became unbearable to her. At that point, she would complain to Calvin.

2. Upon hearing Robbie's complaint, Calvin would logically explain away her grievance in a cool and emotionally detached manner.

3. Under the sway of Calvin's logic, Robbie would blame herself and confess that, as always, she was too emotional and had misunderstood the situation.

4. Gaining strength from his one-up position, Calvin would feel confident enough to draw close to Robbie and express his desire for intimacy and affection.

5. In her one-down position, Robbie felt vulnerable and depressed. Calvin's overtures for closeness at this point only seemed to reaffirm her belief that males are bullying and capricious.

6. Reacting to Robbie's coldness, Calvin would get angry and distance himself from her, confirming his belief that females are dangerous and volatile.

After several weeks, the relationship between Robbie and Calvin would warm up sufficiently for Calvin to get stressed by the closeness. This would trigger the same circular dance over another trivial issue. The couple would replay the entire dance in exactly the same fashion as described above. Surprisingly, the dance was so subtle a part of their routine that Robbie and Calvin replicated the pattern for 12 years without ever recognizing what they were doing. They kept repeating the dance, because it regulated the closeness and distance in their relationship, enabling both to manage the anxiety they experienced from these two relational dimensions.

The Pursuer-Distancer Dance

People in our culture usually learn to handle anxiety in one of two ways: by pursuing or distancing (Lerner, 1985). Pursuers reduce or manage anxiety by getting close. They need to talk about feelings, perceptions, problems, and situations that create anxiety. They want to resolve emotional issues quickly, lest those issues obstruct closeness, thus creating more anxiety for them. Pursuers handle anxiety best when they're close to a significant other.

Distancers handle anxiety in just the opposite way. They hesitate to talk about what's bothering them. They distance themselves from significant others, preferring to manage emotional issues by themselves. Distancers tend not to express feelings, thoughts, problems, and perceptions. Pressuring them to do so only increases the anxiety they feel.

The pursuer-distancer dance effectively diminishes anxiety in relationships when it's flexible. I discovered this to be so when my father died of cancer several years ago. He struggled with this disease for five years, sequentially passing through a series of periods when his health got worse, followed by a plateau when he would stabilize. Toward the end, when I recognized there would not be another plateau, the anxiety of his impending death became unbearable. My ability to function in my profession, as well as to participate as a family member, was severely diminished. I was preoccupied with my impending loss and the task of creating a new world without the presence of my father.

My wife noticed the anxiety I felt. It was apparent in my mood, disposition, and behavior. On several occasions, she asked if I wanted to talk about what I was experiencing, and each time I declined her offer. As a distancer, I coped best with the anxiety by retreating into myself, processing the emotions internally. My wife, understanding how a distancer handles stress, didn't press me to talk. On each occasion, she provided the space I needed. After my father's death and in my own time, I felt comfortable enough to talk to my wife about the emotional distress whirling inside.

A year after my father died, my wife's father died suddenly. Carolyn was concluding a teaching assignment in England and arrived at her father's bedside in time for only one brief final conversation. In the following weeks and months, she was absorbed in helping her mother attend to matters necessary for reestablishing her life. During this period, Carolyn's anxiety began to surge as she assisted Mom and processed her own grief. Realizing that she was a pursuer who handled stress by drawing close, I consciously made myself more available so that she could vent her feelings and emotional pain.

As long as the pursuer-distancer dance remains flexible, it permits the people in a relationship to be emotionally present for each other. Each one gets his or her needs met, anxiety is diminished, and the relationship balance is restored. When the pursuer-distancer dance becomes rigid, the people involved do not get their personal needs met and the dance itself becomes a family stressor. This happens when both partners in the dance rigorously stay in their respective roles—the pursuer always pursues and the distancer always distances. In this situation, the dance becomes self-perpetuating, fueled by its own self-generated anxiety, until one of the partners decides to quit.

Consider the experience of Doris and Max. Doris noticed the classic symptoms of Max's distancing. He became withdrawn, disinterested in family activities, and emotionally detached from family members. He complained of having no energy and seemed down most of the time. Preoccupied with his own thoughts, Max sometimes didn't hear remarks that were directed to him. On other occasions, he'd give glib responses, punctuated with flickers of irritability and exasperation.

Doris responded to Max's distancing with heightened anxiety. She attempted to reduce her anxiety by pressuring Max to talk about what was bothering him—a strategy that only amplified his anxiety, causing him to distance even more. In turn, this increased Doris's anxiety, prompting more efforts on her part to draw close by talking. This pattern continued for several months. Each time Doris attempted to move closer, Max felt smothered and distanced more. Every time Max distanced, Doris felt rejected and pursued more. This dance continued until Doris grew tired of being rejected. Reacting to Max's behavior, she finally distanced herself, instead of pursuing. The consequent space between them emotionally insulated Doris, protecting her from the pain of Max's rejection.

From his viewpoint, Max did not see his own distancing as rejection. He experienced Doris's efforts to draw closer as an invasion of his private space. Fearful of being smothered, he distanced to a position where he felt emotionally comfortable. If Doris and Max had understood the dynamics of their particular dance, as well as the needs of pursuers and distancers, they might have negotiated some changes enabling them to avert the impasse in their relationship. As it was, they neither understood the dance, nor were they in touch with each other's needs. For this reason, their dance became rigid, resulting in Doris's misperception that she was rejected and Max's fear of being smothered.

Although Doris and Max's dance resulted in a chronic impasse, other couples inadvertently have a different experience. When a pursuer tires of pursuing, as Doris did, and distances instead, the other partner in the dance frequently feels secure enough to stop distancing and moves closer. When this happens unconsciously, however, with the couple remaining unaware of the dance, the positive result is usually temporary. Such couples will continue to repeat the entire pattern, with the pursuer becoming exasperated and retreating before the distancer moves closer. Over time, this will produce an excessive level of discontent in their relationship. When couples understand the dynamics of the pursuer-distancer dance, and develop a workable strategy for managing that dance, they are more likely to achieve higher levels of satisfaction in their relationship.

The Overfunction-Underfunction Dance

In healthy relationships, each person invests an equal amount of life energy. Given the nature of relationships, however, two people cannot always invest an equal amount of energy. When the inevitable stressors of life unbalance a relationship, some people resort to an overfunction-underfunction dance to manage the resultant anxiety and restore homeostasis (Lerner, 1989; Kerr and Bowen, 1988). As long as it remains flexible, this dance effectively restores balance. Yet, as with other dances, whenever this dance becomes rigid, it loses its potency to reduce anxiety and becomes a stressor instead. This dance is flexible when the overfunctioning and underfunctioning positions can change with differing circumstances. The dance is rigid when one person always plays the overfunctioning role and the other person always underfunctions.

A flexible version of this dance can be illustrated by returning to the anecdote about my father. In the weeks prior to his death, I invested an increasing amount of time in our relationship. I spoke to him more often by phone and I visited him more frequently. The time I spent with my father was taken from the time I usually spent with my family. While I was visiting my father, I was unable to perform my tasks at home—in other words, I underfunctioned in our family. To keep the household running smoothly, my wife had to overfunction, performing her own family responsibilities as well as mine. A year later, when Carolyn was absorbed with the after-effects of her own father's death, she took time away from her usual family obligations, assuming the role of an underfunctioner at home. To maintain family balance, I performed my own tasks as well as hers, placing myself in the overfunctioner position. Whenever the overfunction-underfunction dance is flexible, it allows the family to function normally even while under stress.

Tad and Betsy portray the devastating effects of a rigid version of this dance, where each person always occupies the same role. Tad was a typical underfunctioner. He reasoned that his vocation outside the home exempted him from domestic responsibilities. Consequently, he did very little around the house. After work and on weekends, he spent his leisure hours watching TV or playing golf with his friends. Betsy, on the other hand, picked up the slack and did almost everything. She was the primary caretaker of their four children, driving them to music lessons and athletic practice, checking their homework assignments, overseeing their household tasks, taking them to doctor and dental appointments, helping them shop for school clothes, and so forth. Betsy also did all the cooking, washing, and cleaning for the family, including retrieving Tad's dirty dishes from the den or picking up his tools if he performed some task around the house. She even helped her son cut the grass and tend the yard. In addition to all this, Betsy had a full-time job outside the home.

Tad and Betsy occupied their respective roles in the overfunction-underfunction dance from the beginning of their marriage. Their roles were seldom mitigated. After 15 years of marriage, Betsy became chronically angry and admitted that she no longer loved her husband.

Although Betsy blamed Tad for the plight of their relationship, the troubled marriage actually resulted from their joint actions. As long as Betsy overfunctioned, she enabled Tad to underfunction. As long as Tad underfunctioned, he forced Betsy to overfunction. Being mutually reinforced, their rigid pattern prevailed across the years until Betsy got fed up and left the marriage.

The Drifting Couple Dance

Some couples manage relationship anxiety by drifting apart over time. This dance is a special favorite of couples who separately fear addressing emotional issues. Rather than negotiate conflicts and differences that obstruct alliances, such individuals are content to leave these matters untouched, which results in an unavoidable drift in their relationship.

Although the drifting couple dance usually involves spouses, it can be played by a parent-child or sibling dyad, whose members drift apart to the point of relinquishing a close and lasting alliance. The dance is particularly well suited for two distancers who feel uncomfortable with closeness. As long as the drifting couple dance is flexible and temporary, it can be an efficient antidote to relationship anxiety. Given the right circumstances, two partners can profitably spend time apart to allow anxiety in their relationship to subside. If the dance is only temporary, the two people will subsequently draw closer to each other. But if the drifting couple dance is rigid and chronic, it usually results in the end of the relationship.

In high school and college, Roger was a star athlete. He never lost his love for sports as he grew older. Athletics continued to be his main focus of attention apart from work. Driven by this enthusiasm, Roger pressured his son, Jason, to be an athlete, even though Jason was not particularly interested in sports, and only participated to humor his father. Jason played football and basketball in middle school, and was on the track team. He was also a member of the community swim team during the summer months. He had to be an athlete if he wanted to have any relationship at all with his dad.

After a while, though, Jason's interest in biology asserted itself. Prior to his senior year in high school, Jason applied for an internship with the Department of Fish and Wildlife. When he was accepted for the job, he decided to drop out of sports altogether. Roger was infuriated when he heard about Jason's decision, and ranted and raved about how stupid it was. He charged his son with being disloyal to the family tradition of males being athletes. Jason was just as rigid as his father in defending his decision to work for Fish and Wildlife as a first step toward a career in biology.

Over a period of several days, the anxiety generated by their struggle became so intense that each distanced from the other. Dad stopped talking to Jason and ignored him when they crossed paths in the house. Jason felt that his father was being incredibly unfair, and appealed to his mother to intervene. After several days of silence in the house, Roger cooled off enough to entertain the idea that perhaps his son was entitled to his own interests. Both wanted a relationship, and were willing to see what compromises they could make to find a common ground. Jason pointed out that his new job would afford them lots of opportunity to go hiking and fishing together.

The interaction between Roger and Jason shows how the drifting couple dance can dispel high levels of anxiety when the dance is temporary. It provided space for both Roger and Jason to emotionally process a decision that disrupted family balance and harmony. As a result of the hiatus in their relationship, both father and son were able to accommodate Jason's decision in a healthier way, providing them an opportunity to restructure their relationship around personal values and issues rather that athletics.

The drifting couple dance was less productive for Clyde and Tilly than it was for Roger and Jason. Clyde and Tilly had been married for only a year when they began drifting apart. They'd had a very brief courtship and during the first year of marriage discovered how little they had in common. Because their interests and values were so disparate, they had one conflict after another, with each partner attempting to impose his or her way on the other. The constant bickering made life unbearable for both Clyde and Tilly, and in time they began drifting apart. In the beginning, the distancing involved only activities, with each spouse doing things alone or with friends. Clyde began spending more time at work, as well as golfing and boating on weekends with some friends who shared his fondness for these activities. Tilly joined several community organizations and became a volunteer at the local hospital. The two would share stories of their day with each other at dinner or while sitting in the den, but even that began to wane in time, as each was so obviously bored by what the other had to say. They finally stopped even sharing meals together (Clyde loved meat, and Tilly was a vegetarian). Clyde moved into the spare bedroom and watched TV there whenever he was at home. After months of living separately under the same roof, both decided that it was in their best interest to divorce. The drifting dance, which originally reduced the anxiety in their relationship, became rigid and chronic, resulting in the demise of their marriage.

The Conflictual Couple Dance

In a pattern opposite to the drifting dance, some couples manage anxiety in their relationship with conflict—in other words, they bicker as a way to mediate closeness when closeness becomes uncomfortable. Conflicts can focus on any issue, whether serious or trivial. Particular issues are only important in that they present an opportunity for the partners to lock horns. This dance enables a couple to calibrate their relationship to an emotionally comfortable position. They can distance when closeness creates an intolerable degree of anxiety, yet they can remain connected or draw closer when the amount of distance between them grows too great. This is the fascinating nature of the conflictual dance. Conflict creates distance, yet simultaneously keeps two people connected.

Emma and Paul each entered their marriage with unresolved issues having to do with their parents. Consequently, both felt uncomfortable with closeness. Each had a high need for individuality and felt smothered when the relationship was going well. Whenever this happened, one or the other would unconsciously trigger an argument over some matter. Paul would define his own position and defend it rigorously. Emma would do the same. After a salubrious dose of conflict, each partner would retreat. Emma usually went to her bedroom, while Paul marched into the den. Although both were angry, each one felt more comfortable cushioned by the newly created distance.

Following the distancing, Emma and Paul's interactions would be civil, but chilly and low-key. After several weeks of this, Emma's anxiety rose as the distance increased between her and Paul. This precipitated another argument, which led to kissing and making up. As a result of their reconciliation, both Paul and Emma enjoyed a feeling of closeness and intimacy. This situation continued until one or the other became uneasy with the amount of closeness. At that point, another argument would ensue, and the whole dance repeated itself.

Emma and Paul participated in the conflictual dance for eight years before they noticed how unbalanced their relationship was. Because they were emotionally stuck in this pattern, neither partner was aware of the dance, or the extent to which it was damaging their marriage. Finally, they went to a therapist for help. A good observer, the therapist was able to discern and then explain the cyclical pattern of the dance to them. They discussed its harmful impact on the marriage. With the therapist's guidance, Emma and Paul learned how to get their needs for distance met without resorting to conflict, as well as how to resolve a legitimate conflict whenever it arose.

Whenever the conflictual dance is flexible, it can be an effective tool for managing relationship anxiety, as long as the couple involved has the skills necessary to negotiate compromises when conflicts arise. This is because conflicts often focus upon a snag in the relationship (Pittman, 1987). Left unattended, such snags tend to get worse over time, contributing to much larger problems. If the snags are identified and resolved, a relationship can be both strengthened and enhanced. A couple must possess the ability to resolve conflict if their relationship is to prosper.

The Nature of Dances

Dances are indigenous to all family relationships. Various dyads in the family may use different dances, or even the same one with different partners. Families give their own distinctive stamp to how a dance is conducted or how long it is used. But dances are present in all relationships, and the nature of the basic types of dances is always the same. Relationship dances are always composed of five common elements.

1. All relationship dances are attempts to reduce anxiety in the partners and restore balance to their relationship. Anxiety, or stress, from any origin tends to unbalance an alliance between two people. Under stress, the partners don't get along as well and tend not to behave in ways that meet each other's needs. When a stressful situation arises, the partners will automatically and unconsciously engage in one of the dances you've just read about. The dance will be used to reduce the anxiety of both people involved and restore balance, or homeostasis, to their relationship. As long as the dance is flexible and temporary, it produces desirable relief. If the dance becomes chronic and inflexible, with each person always occupying the same position, the dance loses its potency to reduce anxiety and itself becomes a stressor for the relationship.

2. All relationship dances protect a couple from anxiety they think they might experience if there is a change in the rules of their partnership. Suppose, for example, that Clyde and Tilly, the couple whose marriage was doomed by the drifting couple dance, decided to go to a marriage counselor instead of getting a divorce. During the first weeks of therapy, both vigorously resisted the therapist's efforts to stimulate positive change in their marriage. In spite of every suggestion, they continued the distancing dance. If Clyde and Tilly were to be candid with themselves, they might admit their fear of change. To be sure, their present marriage arrangement is uncomfortable; but neither knows what will happen if they create a different kind of relationship. Will the marriage survive the change? Will both partners be able to do what is necessary to maintain the changes? Will each spouse have to sacrifice too much in a new, workable relationship? Will they be satisfied with the results? The fear generated by such questions caused Clyde and Tilly to maintain the uncomfortable alliance forged by their distancing dance. Even though it was dysfunctional in every other way, the dance protected them from their anxiety about change.

Couples commonly experience fear about changes in their relationship, becoming anxious about what will happen if their alliance is altered. Many couples resist change, perpetuating even dysfunctional behavioral patterns rather than make changes that might improve their relationship. The dances described here provide protection from the fear of change by maintaining the status quo in relationships.

3. In all the relationship dances, the partners involved provoke and reinforce each other's behavior. When, for instance, a wife or mother overfunctions in a relationship, she provokes her husband or child to underfunction. This reinforces the woman's belief that she needs to overfunction to take up the slack. The more energetic the overfunctioner becomes, the more she reinforces and provokes her partner in the dance to underfunction. It's a vicious cycle of reinforcement. This process works the same in all relationship dances. For this reason, blaming or accusing one person for his or her part in a dance is both meaningless and futile. Dancing always involves the cooperation of both partners. Each one stimulates and reinforces the behavior of the other.

4. Because dances involve mutually reinforcing behavior, any dance can be broken, or terminated, by either participant. As long as both partners continue their particular behavior in the dance, it goes on. It only takes one person to end the dance by deciding to change his or her role. Each partner always responds to the other's action. When one dancer does something differently, the other will have to respond differently. Whether this response enhances or diminishes the relationship, the dance is altered, and so is the behavior of both partners. What happens, for example, if a wife stops overfunctioning for her underfunctioning husband? When the husband can no longer depend on his wife to do this or that for him, he will have to do it himself or get someone else to do his dirty work. In either case, he must change his underfunctioning role in relation to his wife, because she is no longer in the dance. Her change of behavior has forced a change on his part as well.

5. In all relationship dances, one person's behavioral change will evoke a countermove by their partner. A countermove is a conscious or unconscious response intended to pressure agents of change back into their accustomed role in the dance (Lerner, 1985).

For years, Carolyn overfunctioned for her husband, Phil, doing such tasks as picking up his dirty clothes and putting them in the clothes hamper. To deal with her anger stemming from this situation, Carolyn announced one day that she would no longer put Phil's dirty clothes in the hamper. If he didn't pick up after himself, his clothes would simply pile up on the bedroom floor, and wouldn't be washed when the other laundry was done.

Phil didn't appreciate Carolyn's ultimatum, and made numerous complaints. When the complaints didn't force his wife from her new position, Phil tried manipulating her with guilt, telling her that it was a wife's duty to pick up after her husband. When this didn't work, he threw tantrums and made threats about leaving her if she didn't pick up his clothes.

Carolyn told Phil that she agreed with him: the situation had gotten out of hand. The smell in the bedroom was so bad that she could hardly sleep. She told Phil not to worry—whenever she found his clothes on the floor or draped over a chair from now on, she'd simply throw them out.

Well, Phil was a man who liked his clothes—at least, he knew that he couldn't afford to buy a new wardrobe every week. He thought at first that Carolyn was bluffing; but when he took out the garbage one day and saw his favorite polo shirt there at the top of the can with the banana skins and soggy cardboard, he realized that he was just going to have to change.

Even though Phil didn't rationally plan a campaign of complaints, guilt inculcation, tantrums, and threats, all of these were countermoves designed to coerce Carolyn back into her overfunctioning role. This kind of automatic reaction happens whenever one partner changes his or her role in a relationship dance. The change of role produces anxiety in the other person, who tries to force things back to the status quo. If the partner who changed acquiesces and resumes his or her usual role, the stress level of the other partner is lowered, and homeostasis is restored. If the trail-blazing partner insists on maintaining the change, the other person will employ any number of countermoves to resist it. If none of these attempts work, change is forced on the partner who wanted to keep on dancing in the old familiar way.

Exercise

This exercise is designed to help you identify and assess the various dances you practice in your significant relationships.

Step 1: Identifying Your Dances

You can organize information about the dance, or dances you use by completing the table at the end of this chapter. Your understanding of how you typically respond to others in stressful situations will be greater if you include all of your significant relationships in the inventory. Here are some instructions:

- In the RELATIONSHIP column, note the specific relationships that you consider to be significant.

- In the ISSUE column, identify the issues that chronically trigger higher levels of anxiety of stress—the issues that never seem to get resolved.

- In the DANCE column, describe the part you play in any given dance (i.e., distance, overfunction), or just name the dance itself (i.e., conflictual couple).

- In the FLEXIBILITY column, rate the rigidity or flexibility of the dance on a 1 to 10 scale, with 1 being extremely rigid and 10 being extremely flexible.

- In the OUTCOME column, note whether the dance reduces anxiety associated with the issue, and whether or not the dance usually succeeds in restoring balance in the relationship.

On the next page is an example of a chart that was filled in by Ann, a 33-year-old woman who lives with her husband, 9-year-old son, and her mother, who is recuperating from a coronary illness.

Step 2: Analysing Your Dances

When Ann charted the dances she used in handling stressful issues with the significant people in her life, she immediately recognized a primary source of the anxiety she had been feeling for the past two months. The chart provided a global view of the dances she was using, as well as an indication that most of these dances were ineffectual in reducing the stress in her life. This helped her gain several insights. Ann's overfunctioning was enabling her mother to underfunction so far as accepting responsibility for taking her own medicine. In terms of her husband, Ann had been aware that they frequently argued over finances; but she was unaware of the conflictual dance that prevented them from resolving that issue. She also realized that the circular dance with her son simultaneously reinforced his resistance to do homework and provided a way for him to get more attention from her. By completing this assessment, Ann gained a clearer perspective about specific ways in which she might change her part in the dances with members of her family. She had no power to change what the others were doing; yet she could share her perceptions with them and ask for their cooperation in getting rid of the ineffectual dances. Ann understood that she had the power to change her own part in those dances, whatever the others decided to do.

After you've filled out the chart to show your own dances and stressful issues, you're ready to do an analysis. Use a separate sheet of paper for this part of the exercise.

Relationship	Issue	Dance	Flexibility 1-10	Outcome
Husband	(1) Talk about personal problems	Pursuer	5	Moderately successful—he often listens and responds
	(2) When he's caring for his ailing father	Over-function	7	Good result—enables us to cope well
	(3) Household expenses	Conflictual couple	1	Never gets resolved, but I get indigestion
Son	Doing homework	Circular	3	Seldom works—anxiety remains high and I put myself down as an ineffective parent
Mother	Oversee her medications	Over-function	4	Seldom works—she won't accept personal responsibility and I get irritated

- Isolate the ineffectual dances. Those with a high level of rigidity and undesirable outcomes are usually ineffectual.

- List the factors that make a given dance ineffectual.

- List your behaviors that reinforce and maintain the dance.

Step 3: Planning for Change

If you've found that there are dances you want to change, you can use these strategies:

- Express your desire to change a dance to other people who are involved. Explain how your behavior and your partner's fits one of the descriptions of dances given earlier in this chapter (refer to the definitions in this book if you want to). In a nonblaming way, be specific about why you no longer want to follow the same routine. Ask for your dance partner's cooperation in changing the dance.

- If the other person refuses to participate in changing the dance, you still have the option of changing on your own. Remember that it only takes one person to alter a dance pattern. If you decide to change, make a list for yourself of the specific behaviors that will change your role in the dance. Mentally rehearse these behaviors so that you'll be able to implement them whenever the dance recurs.

- Write down what you will say or do if the other person attempts to countermove you back into your original position in the dance. Remember that when you change your part in a dance, the other person will also change, since the dance no longer goes on as usual. There is no way to know beforehand, unfortunately, whether the other person will change his or her behavior in a positive way. Your only guarantee is that you *will* bring about a change.

Summary

1. Over time, all emotionally significant relationships are unbalanced by anxiety from a variety of sources. When a relationship is un-

balanced, interactions between the partners are stymied, and their individual needs go unmet.

2. Partners in a relationship manage stress by using repetitive behaviors called dances. The major relationship dances are the circular dance, the pursuer-distancer dance, the overfunction-underfunction dance, the drifting couple dance, and the conflictual dance.

3. *The circular dance* is composed of mutually reinforcing behaviors on the part of two people when each one always takes the same position, says the same words, and does the same thing whenever a particular situation or issue arises.

4. *The pursuer-distancer* dance involves dissonant ways of handling anxiety. Pursuers reduce relationship anxiety by drawing close to their partner, talking out problems and feelings, and openly addressing issues creating the anxiety. Distancers move away from the relationship, preferring not to talk about issues or feelings. Distancers reduce relationship anxiety by creating and maintaining emotional space.

5. *The overfunction-underfunction dance* calls for one person to overfunction in a relationship and the other to underfunction. Overfunctioners do more than their share of physical and emotional work in maintaining an alliance. Underfunctioners respond by doing less than their share.

6. *The drifting couple dance* involves two people who distance from each other when anxiety levels in the relationship are high.

7. *The conflictual couple dance* is performed by couples who manage relationship anxiety through conflict. Conflict produces the emotional distance that both people need, and simultaneously keeps them connected to each other.

8. As long as relationship dances are temporary and flexible in terms of who plays which role, they can be effective tools for reducing relationship anxiety. When the dances are chronic and rigid, with the same person always playing the same role, they lose their ability to reduce relationship anxiety and themselves become stressors in the relationship.

9. The purpose of relationship dances is to reduce anxiety and restore homeostasis in the relationship.

10. Relationship dances protect people from the anxiety they think they might experience if the relationship changed.

11. In all relationship dances, each person stimulates and reinforces the other's behavior. Each dance is a cooperative venture.

12. Relationship dances may be broken, or terminated, by either person in the alliance. When one person in an alliance changes, the other must also change. Such changes can have either a positive or negative effect on the relationship.

13. Whenever one person changes his or her dance pattern, the other person in the alliance will countermove automatically to restore the customary pattern.

14. Relationship dances can be performed by any pair of people in a family, including a spousal dyad, a sibling dyad, or a parent-child dyad.

References

Kerr, M. E., and M. Bowen (1988) *Family Evaluation.* New York: W.W. Norton & Co.

Lerner, H. G. (1985) *The Dance of Anger.* New York: Harper & Row.

Lerner, H. G. (1989) *The Dance of Intimacy.* New York: Harper & Row.

Pittman, F. S. (1987) *Turning Points.* New York: W.W. Norton & Co.

Relationship	Issue	Dance	Flexibility 1-10	Outcome

8

On Being Responsible
for Yourself

The myth of Orestes was a popular story among the ancient Greeks. Orestes was the son of Agamemnon and Clytemnestra. With the help of an accomplice, Clytemnestra murdered her husband. This crime propelled Orestes into a tangled dilemma—for, according to Greek custom, a son was obligated to slay his father's murderer. This obligation was complicated for Orestes, because Greek custom also designated matricide as the greatest wrong a person could commit. Orestes agonized over his dilemma, but finally decide to avenge his father's death by killing his mother.

The gods punished Orestes by plaguing him with three Furies, demons from the underworld. The Furies were loathsome creatures who could be heard and seen only by Orestes. They haunted him everywhere he traveled, tormenting him day and night with their horrendous antics. After may years of misery, Orestes petitioned the gods for absolution. He was repentant for killing his mother and believed he had suffered enough.

So the gods held another trial for Orestes. Speaking in his defense, Apollo argued that Orestes should not be held accountable for his deed, since he, Apollo, had created the situation in which Orestes had no other choice but to kill his mother. At this point, Orestes interrupted Apollo and exclaimed, "It was I, not Apollo, who killed my mother!"

The gods were astonished by Orestes's words. They were impressed that he accepted responsibility for his action, rather than blaming the gods. Consequently, they rescinded his punishment. They removed the Furies who had tormented Orestes over the years, and replaced them with the Eumenides, the "grace bearers." The Eumenides brought good fortune to Orestes.

Orestes is a model for people who would transform a life of private hell into one of grace and well-being. Orestes could have blamed the gods for his predicament, but he rejected this tactic, preferring to accept personal responsibility for his own misery. In the same fashion, you might blame your family, or society, or others, or fate, for whatever distress plagues your own life course. Yet one cannot do this in good conscience. No matter how traumatic your family experiences may have been, you are responsible for yourself and the life you choose to live. Beginning as a young child, you have always decided how to respond to situations you encounter, and these decisions have shaped your personality. It is for this reason that the journey to discover your personal identity will always lead back to yourself. You have the final word on who you really are.

Human Nature

There are two prominent theories that attempt to solve the puzzle of human character. One theory proposes that *essence determines existence*. This proposition assumes that people possess an inner essence which constitutes their true self. A popular corollary conjecture rooted in this proposition is that human beings cannot change, that they are the way they are and that's that. As Plato once said, "The soul knows who we are from the beginning." This theory also affirms that your essence, or inner nature, governs your existence—how you live from day to day.

On the surface, this theory has substance. Individuals all have certain inherent elements that determine how they behave. Each human being has millions of genes composed of his or her parents' particular DNA. This genetic imprinting influences a myriad of your abilities, traits, and characteristics. DNA influences much more that just physical qualities: researchers are now discovering that genetic make-up predisposes people to a wide range of behaviors, including those peculiar to serious mental illnesses, alcoholism, and perhaps even sexual preference. To some extent, you do have an inner nature, or essence, that determines your existence. But is this the whole truth?

Another theory proposes that *existence determines essence.* This view assumes that your existence, the way in which you live and behave, shapes who you become: in other words, your essence. This theory is also compelling. Consider the numerous self-improvement programs peddled in the media. If you want to build a healthier body, or cultivate the ability to get along with people, or become a stupendous salesperson, or lose weight, or stop smoking, or learn French, there is a program designed with you in mind. Such self-improvement programs usually follow a before-and-after format. They show you how to span the gap between the way you are now and the way you'll be when you're new and improved. First, you make a choice. You *decide* to change in some way. Then you follow a program. You scrupulously adhere to a rigorous plan of action, so that someday in the future you will achieve your intended goal.

You'll notice in this scenario that you achieve your goal for changing this or that about yourself because you *do* something. You make choices and behave in certain ways. In this manner, *existence—*what you do—determines *essence—*who you become: you have an innate ability to change yourself. And if you can change yourself, you can determine, to some extent, who you are.

These two theories would seem to be contradictory. Which one correctly describes the nature of human existence? In fact, they both do. The two seemingly contradictory theories are actually complimentary; they simply view the human experience from two different angles. As an individual, you have a given essence that influences your existence in many ways. Who you are determines how you live.

The opposite is also true. How you live also shapes who you are: your existence molds your essence.

Being and Doing

Because you have an essence, you can speak of yourself as a human *being*. Yet, because you freely make choices and behave in ways that mold who you are, you can also speak of yourself in terms of human *doings*. You can never separate yourself from what you do, and you are always doing something, even when you're sleeping. This is true to such an extent that you *are* what you *do*. More accurately, you are what you're doing at any given moment.

If someone entered the room where you are reading these words, and asked, "What are you doing?", you would probably respond, "I'm reading." Notice the question and the answer. The question asks about *doing*. Your answer defines who you are, "I *am* reading." Although this is in part simply a peculiarity of English grammar, it's also true that while you are reading, you *are* reading. You are what you are doing at the moment. When you lay the book aside and walk away, you will no longer *be* a reader. You will then *be* a walker—if someone asks you what you are doing, you will say, "I'm walking." And if it's raining outside and you begin running to another place, you will say, if asked, "I'm running." And so it goes. You can never separate what you are doing at any particular moment from who you are. You *are* what you *do*.

Because you are a "human doing" as well as a human being, identifying yourself involves observing how you behave. Who am I? When I am writing, I am a writer. When I am speaking, I am a speaker. When I am thinking, I am a thinker. When I am relaxing, I am a relaxer. I am always doing something, even when I'm doing nothing, and what I'm doing is a partial definition of who I am. The same is true for you.

The *doing* facet of personal identity is not a new concept. It is merely a concept that largely has been ignored in Western civilization. This is because our basic world view has been influenced by Greek philosophy, a way of thinking that focuses upon categories, being, and essence. The Judeo-Christian elements of our culture, however, represent a basic world view which is common to Eastern civilization. According to this view, nature is dynamic, always moving and changing.

This is why, in Jewish and Christian literature, people are defined by their behavior.

On one occasion, Jesus, the founder of Christianity, was asked by one of John the Baptist's disciples if he was indeed the Messiah. Jesus did not provide a yes or no answer. He was a Jew, an Easterner, and did not use Greek concepts of categories, being and essence. He answered the disciple, "Go and tell John what you are seeing and hearing: the lame walk, lepers are healed, the deaf hear, the dead are raised up, and the poor have the gospel preached to them" (Matthew 11:4-5). In this situation, Jesus identified himself by what he was doing. His actions defined who he was. This connection between being and doing pervades all of the ancient Jewish and Christian writings, and it is inherent in all other Eastern religions as well.

Assuming that you are what you do, your individual nature is nothing more than characteristic behavior. The words someone might use to characterize you express belief that result from how you usually behave. If someone says you are friendly, that person is expressing a belief based on how you characteristically behave. If someone describes you as being kind, he or she is characterizing you on the basis of how you usually act. Think about the dominant characteristics of your closest friend. In all probability, most of these characteristics describe how your friend typically behaves. Our nature does not wholly reside inside us. A measure of our nature is defined by the way we normally act.

The observation that your identity is somehow connected to your behavior is highly significant in the search for yourself. If you believe that there is a fully developed *self* buried somewhere deep inside your psyche, you are likely never to discover yourself. That idea is an illusion. You do have an inner essence, yet that essence is not all of you. Attempting to find your real self by peeling away numerous layers of your unconscious and uncovering your hidden self is like stripping away the layers of an onion to find the onion inside. The real onion is not there, because the onion is merely a series of layers encrusted around one another. In similar fashion, there is not a fully developed but unrecognized self inside of you. In actuality, you are a fusion of energies, comprised of constantly moving biological systems, cognitive activities, arbitrary choices, and behavioral responses, all fueled by your genetic heritage. All of these collectively, like a magnificent stained-glass window created from thousands of smaller pieces, comprise a unique and Promethean *self* who happens to be you.

Doing and Becoming

There are several dimensions to personhood. The physical dimension is the most obvious; but besides this, you also have an emotional dimension, a social dimension, a cognitive dimension, a spiritual dimension, and a volitional dimension. Volition enables you to make choices. This dimension empowers you to *will* certain things into being, not the least of which is your identity.

What do you want to be like when you are old? I know one older person who is as obstinate and grouchy as he is lovable. He observes nothing beautiful or wonderful about the world. He criticizes everyone and is pleased by nothing. He's married to one of the most congenial and agreeable women this side of sainthood. She never complains, and looks for a silver lining in every ominous cloud. Rather than whine about gloomy events, she takes the initiative in making good things happen. Although she is in her eighties, this woman keeps herself alive by learning about novel ideas and pursuing new adventures.

When you become 80 years old, would you rather be like the husband or the wife? The person you become will be no accident. You are sculpting that person today. Just as you are now the product of all you have experienced, so who you become tomorrow will result from what you do today. Your identity has not only been shaped, it is being shaped by how you live. The lady mentioned above is alive and vibrant today because she lived that way yesterday. The quality of her husband's life is diminished because he lived the way he has become. In this manner, people are always giving birth to themselves. Show me how you are living now and I will know who you will become in the future. In large measure, your identity is your own doing.

And so, after researching family roles, scripts, and rules, what will you do with the data you've compiled? After meandering through the labyrinth of your family origins, and traversing the rugged terrain and secret passages of your own inner being, how does the quest for yourself end?

The outcome of your quest, like the journey itself, is up to you. Even if you would like to abdicate the responsibility, you are the only one who can discover yourself. You are the only one who can decide who you are and who you will become. This is an open secret which many people ignore. Your true self is not a completed entity which resides inside your being. Your true self is still in the process of being created, and you are in charge of that process.

In response to Socrates' maxim to "Know thyself," S. Kierke-gaard was on target when he affirmed that a person's prior obligation is to "Choose thyself" (Arbaugh and Arbaugh, 1967). Choosing your-self requires the freedom to commit yourself to who you truly are, to take responsibility for yourself. Like Orestes, you must accept respon-sibility for all of your decisions and past actions. You are responsible for the life course you are now living. Only when you accept this responsibility can you be liberated from your personal Furies.

You must also assume control of your decisions and actions from this point on. Claiming responsibility for yourself means that you define your own thoughts, beliefs, feelings, ideals, values, and behavior, rather than permitting these to be determined by your en-vironment. Personal responsibility involves defining yourself for others, deciding for yourself what you will do or not do, rather than granting others the power to decide for you. Being responsible for yourself means resolving toxic issues with your original family and claiming your own participation in that family system. Being respon-sible for yourself means deciding now to live creatively, no longer re-playing old patterns that diminish and restrict your existence. When you choose to be the self you truly are, instead of confusing yourself with old roles and scripts, your personal demons will be transformed into bearers of grace, enabling you to experience a new way of being.

Sam Keen quotes Carl G. Jung as once remarking that his most pressing task was to discover the unconscious myth that he was living (Keen, 1989). He was not alone in that venture. This is an essential goal for all people who yearn to become themselves rather than per-petuate a worn-out script that gnarls, inhibits, or distorts aspects of their own personal uniqueness. Discovering your authentic self, the person enveloped in the unconscious life script, or myth, that you are living, and amassing the courage to be that person, are two of the most crucial tasks you will ever undertake. This truth is succinctly reflected in a legion from an ancient Coptic manuscript of the Gospel of Thomas:

"If you bring forth what is within you,
what you bring forth will make you whole.
If you do not bring forth what is within you,
what you do not bring forth
will destroy you."

References

Arbaugh, G. E., and G. B. Arbaugh, (1967) *Kierkegaard's Authorship*. Rock Island, IL: Augustana College Library.

Keen, S., and A. Valley-Fox, (1989) *Your Mythic Journey*. Los Angeles: Jeremy P. Tarcher

Rogers, Carl R. (1961) *On Becoming a Person*. Boston: Houghton-Mifflin Co.

Other New Harbinger Self-Help Titles

Father-Son Healing: An Adult Son's Guide, $12.95
The Chemotherapy Survival Guide, $11.95
Your Family/Your Self: How to Analyze Your Family System, $11.95
Being a Man: A Guide to the New Masculinity, $12.95
The Deadly Diet, Second Edition: Recovering from Anorexia & Bulimia, $11.95
Last Touch: Preparing for a Parent's Death, $11.95
Consuming Passions: Help for Compulsive Shoppers, $11.95
Self-Esteem, Second Edition, $12.95
Depression & Anxiety Mangement: An audio tape for managing emotional problems, $11.95
I Can't Get Over It, A Handbook for Trauma Survivors, $12.95
Concerned Intervention, When Your Loved One Won't Quit Alcohol or Drugs, $11.95
Redefining Mr. Right, $11.95
Dying of Embarrassment: Help for Social Anxiety and Social Phobia, $11.95
The Depression Workbook: Living With Depression and Manic Depression, $13.95
Risk-Taking for Personal Growth: A Step-by-Step Workbook, $11.95
The Marriage Bed: Renewing Love, Friendship, Trust, and Romance, $11.95
Focal Group Psychotherapy: For Mental Health Professionals, $44.95
Hot Water Therapy: Save Your Back, Neck & Shoulders in 10 Minutes a Day $11.95
Older & Wiser: A Workbook for Coping With Aging, $12.95
Prisoners of Belief: Exposing & Changing Beliefs that Control Your Life, $10.95
Be Sick Well: A Healthy Approach to Chronic Illness, $11.95
Men & Grief: A Guide for Men Surviving the Death of a Loved One., $11.95
When the Bough Breaks: A Helping Guide for Parents of Sexually Abused Childern, $11.95
Love Addiction: A Guide to Emotional Independence, $11.95
When Once Is Not Enough: Help for Obsessive Compulsives, $11.95
The New Three Minute Meditator, $9.95
Getting to Sleep, $10.95
The Relaxation & Stress Reduction Workbook, 3rd Edition, $13.95
Leader's Guide to the Relaxation & Stress Reduction Workbook, $19.95
Beyond Grief: A Guide for Recovering from the Death of a Loved One, $10.95
Thoughts & Feelings: The Art of Cognitive Stress Intervention, $13.95
Messages: The Communication Skills Book, $12.95
The Divorce Book, $11.95
Hypnosis for Change: A Manual of Proven Techniques, 2nd Edition, $12.95
The Chronic Pain Control Workbook, $13.95
Rekindling Desire: Bringing Your Sexual Relationship Back to Life, $12.95
Visualization for Change, $12.95
Videotape: Clinical Hypnosis for Stress & Anxiety Reduction, $24.95
Starting Out Right: Essential Parenting Skills for Your Child's First Seven Years, $12.95
Big Kids: A Parents' Guide to Weight Control for Children, $11.95
My Parent's Keeper: Adult Children of the Emotionally Disturbed, $11.95
When Anger Hurts, $12.95
Free of the Shadows: Recovering from Sexual Violence, $12.95
Lifetime Weight Control, $11.95
The Anxiety & Phobia Workbook, $13.95
Love and Renewal: A Couple's Guide to Commitment, $12.95
The Habit Control Workbook, $12.95

Call **toll free, 1-800-748-6273**, to order. Have your Visa or Mastercard number ready. Or send a check for the titles you want to New Harbinger Publications, Inc., 5674 Shattuck Avenue, Oakland, CA 94609. Include $3.80 for the first book and 75¢ for each additional book, to cover shipping and handling. (California residents please include appropriate sales tax.) Allow four to six weeks for delivery.

Prices subject to change without notice.